AFTER THE F

The confidence manual for the n

Practical, realistic advice for the nervous or reluctant competitor, whether you are experienced but suffering from self-doubt or a novice wondering which way to turn or what to do, this book can lead the way and get you on track. Learn how to help overcome your fear and deal effectively with your self-doubt and anxiety while taking small steps to change your mind-set, achieve your goals and enjoy riding your horse for competition, whatever your level or discipline.

H U Owen

Also by H U Owen:
I HOPE IT RAINS... The Confidence Manual for the nervous rider © 2019

Copyright: H U Owen © 2021

The right of H U Owen to be identified as the author of this book has been asserted by her in accordance with the Copyright, Design & Patents Act, 1988.

The moral right of the author has been asserted.

ISBN: 9798746363077

All rights reserved. Apart from any use permitted under UK copyright law, no part of this publication may be reproduced, stored or transmitted in any form or by any means without the prior permission in writing of the publisher or in the case of reprographic production in accordance with the terms of licences issued by the Copyright Licensing Agency.

Every effort has been made to fulfil requirements with regard to reproducing copyright material. The author will be glad to rectify any omission at the earliest opportunity.

Published by H U Owen

DISCLAIMER

If you have had any form of accident or are unsure if you should ride, please do seek medical advice to ensure you are physically fit before riding. Riding is a risk sport and the author accepts no responsibility, whatsoever including but not limited to accident, injury, loss or damage to any animal, person or anything arising from riding or handling any horse or from practising any of the ideas or methods set out herein either directly or indirectly.

PREFACE

It brings me much pleasure that my first book *I Hope It Rains… The Confidence Manual for the nervous rider* (which I am proud to say is an Amazon best seller*) has helped hundreds of riders who have a hit a 'bad patch'. To receive the lovely messages and emails from people around the world who were in the depths of despair, not knowing if they could face riding any longer, telling me how, after following the programme and taking on the suggestions in the book, they were able to overcome their fear and anxiety and re-train themselves to enjoy riding once again, has been the most wonderful reward. Although baring my soul on the page was well intentioned, it is never as easy as one may think. There is always the worry of how well a work will be received, especially in today's judgmental world.

In the same vein, I sincerely hope that this book will do the job of mending the mind-set of the rider, in as much as it will give an understanding of what causes emotional turmoil and how to deal effectively with it so that you are no longer held back by the invisible but immensely powerful prison of your own mind, self-doubt and unease, particularly prevalent during times of pressure. If I can help one person get in the arena or out on the course to enjoy competing, my work is certainly done and I will take great personal comfort knowing that a rider has gone from being too worried to have a go, to taking part and bringing home their first rosette. I sincerely hope that is the case for each and every one of you reading this book and wish you all the luck in the world. I hope you will achieve your goals with your special equine friend. Never give up. After all, today is a great day to start living your dreams and bringing home those well-deserved, hard-earned rosettes.

INTRODUCTION

Confident, brave, self-assured, accomplished. I think people assume that I am many if not all those things on a horse which is a huge compliment. Coupled with doing well in competitions, I guess they assume that I don't have any self-doubt, nerves or worries when competing, never make mistakes, never get it wrong, never get upset with my progress, never mess up and never fall off. Wrong, oh so very wrong! Let's clear that up once and for all. I am not super-human, I am just like most people. I get butterflies before competition and although not all encompassing, I occasionally doubt myself and worry that I'm not good enough or am in some way lacking and of course I make mistakes.

What I have learned is, all of those feelings are normal and exist because I care passionately about what I am doing and want to be the best I can be which, let's be fair, is no bad thing. Oh, yes, I fall off very occasionally too. The difference is, and this is the important part, I know it's *normal* to have the odd 'assisted dismount' as well as feel those different emotions that come as part of riding. Not only do I *understand* but, more importantly, I *accept* it. I have taught myself to cope with those feelings and trained myself to be rational about what it is I am setting out to do and why I want to do it. I weigh up what there is to lose (usually nothing) and what there is to gain (usually a lot) and put it all into perspective so it doesn't overwhelm me and become a burden.

Working with my self-analytical workbooks, which I will show you how to use later in the book, I have learned to break issues down when they arise and deal with problems before they get too big. I see riding as a journey that I embrace with passion and commitment. It is the reason I get up in the morning. I care for my animals and progress my learning whilst schooling, competing and growing as a rider. Rationalising the pros and cons of competing is a very important step, as is relaxation, breathing and other techniques for helping stay focussed and 'bringing down' the emotions to a manageable level. People who don't really understand this approach may well view some techniques they are unfamiliar with or unprepared to try, as a load of mumbo-jumbo, but it's more than just doing a few deep breaths before a competition. That would be no more than a sticking plaster and not deal with the root of the anxiety. Relaxation/breathing is of course important but it has to be coupled with other ways of knowing and understanding where anxiety is coming from, what is REALLY causing you to feel like you do as well as learning the techniques to overcome and cope.

Preparing well for competition is more than just training your horse well. You also need to train your body by being as fit and healthy as you can and to train your mind to deal with the stress this brings out. You could have the best, most well-trained horse in the world but if you are a 'shaky jelly legs' who is so nervous you can't think straight, feel nauseous and your blood-pressure is through the roof, you can't expect to do particularly well until you have mastered controlling those feelings and consequent horrible physical symptoms. You need to put in place strategies to use the nerves to your advantage and bring the whole situation down to a manageable, acceptable level. If you are in such a heightened state of panic and anticipation, on the verge of passing-out or crying, and you can't control it, there is no way you will be able effectively to ride a creature with its own mind, who is sensitive and able to pick-up on your every feeling. Even at the most subtle level the horse will feel your anxiety and wonder why there is 'danger'. He will inevitably start to 'act up' or at least not perform as well as when you are at home or in a less-stressful environment. He will simply act like a horse and, no doubt, become a mirror of you. The old saying "what goes on in the brain, goes down the reins" is very true, so of course you can't be expected to do well in this scenario.

How on earth can you expect to do anything productive, or act in anything like the way needed to get in the arena and do well? You need to work on changing that and this is where this book comes in to help you. It's not your fault that you are feeling anxious, but we need to help you control it to such a degree it is no longer an issue and you can 'see' clearly enough to enjoy competing, at whatever level, and learn how to manage the feelings, lessen the nerves and understand how you can be calmer in competition. This in turn allows you to focus on the task in hand and, ultimately, do better. It's all about understanding yourself, using knowledge gained from the self-analytical workbooks, positive mind-set re-wiring exercises, visualisation, relaxation techniques and working hard to stack the odds in your favour before attempting to compete or move up to a higher level or do a more difficult course. These are the keys to unlock the world you so desperately want to be part of or, should I say, take part in.

Anyone can do these exercises to significantly improve their outlook and chances. It's not just novices who are nervous either. Anyone can feel immense pressure when in the spotlight and for the experienced rider the same techniques are priceless for allowing you to focus and 'up your game' considerably. What's more, save for the purchase of this book, unless you want to enlist the help of a professional sports psychologist or other professional, it's all free. Yes, the suggestions and plans all take a little time to work at and improve, but reading this book is only the start, you have to actually *do* the exercises! The good part is they are not complex, anyone can do them and they are set out in such a way that they are easy to understand and can be tailored to meet your exact personal needs, which is why they are suitable for any rider, in any discipline, at any level.

Look at it this way, reading a recipe book doesn't make the cake, it just shows you the way of doing it, invites you to have a go at baking it yourself. You still have to mix the ingredients together and put it in the oven. In this case, it's the same. Take on board the information and put it into practice, then you will start to see results. Just about anything, within reason, you set your heart on can be accomplished with time and perseverance so expect to do some soul searching. Along with the mental exercises you will start to take control of your nerves and get them down to a manageable level so that they work for you and not against you.

Throughout the book I refer to 'fear and anxiety' for ease of expression. However, in general, 'fear' is a reaction to a specific, observable danger, while 'anxiety' is more an unfocused, objectless, future-oriented, 'what if', worst case scenario kind of feeling. Although the focus of the response is different (real v imagined danger), fear and anxiety are interrelated. When faced with fear, most people will experience the physical reactions that are commonly described under the umbrella of anxiety. Fear can cause anxiety and anxiety can cause fear. So perhaps you will forgive me the descriptive use of both? Let's face it, both emotions feel horrible, so let's not split hairs on clinical definitions but get down to learning to cope with the *feelings* that present in times of stress.

Many competitors, even if they are not wracked with nerves, recognise that they are anxious about something but cannot always put their finger on it. This is why you are going to use a number of techniques including work books in the form of self-analytical lists, to help highlight what is upsetting you and find out more about that specific thing to enable you to identify it, deal with it properly and control better the anxiety around it. The aim here is to free you from the imaginary shackles of anxiousness, one manageable step at a time.

I'm not an Olympic athlete and I'm guessing you aren't either. If we were, I am sure we would have a significant team behind us, coaching, teaching, educating and supporting us emotionally and physically for our all-round well-being, not to mention the army of support for the horse. All of these things are required to succeed at top level and, for most serious athletes, are par for the course. However, even though we are not Olympians, why shouldn't we have a game plan and take part in positive mind-set coaching to achieve the same understanding as sportsmen and women at top level? No one thinks having a riding instructor or a professional trainer is elitist, so if that is acceptable why not think about using the other strategies available to a top rider?

In this book we will look at how anyone, with effort and understanding, can become a stealthy opponent and a confident, happy competitor who competes because they enjoy it but at the same time does well and reaps the rewards that putting in the hard work brings. Success can be yours, you just have to know how to approach it and deal with the journey one day at a time. Time will pass anyway so put it to good use and eventually you will look back, see how far you have come and be proud of all the amazing things you have achieved with your horse.

In the following pages, we shall identify tension and look at the cause. This may be something you are actually not aware of, such as the fear of getting something wrong leading to embarrassment or, as you may describe it, "looking silly in front of others".
We shall discover how to overcome what is commonly termed 'performance anxiety' and learn to understand what the fear is all about. Are you getting upset because you are afraid to disappoint others or think you are not as good as your peers or the people you see on social media? We shall learn how to look at your 'fears' head on, challenge them and rationalise them. What is so important about the dressage test or course of jumps? Will the world really end if you make a mistake?

We shall learn how to embrace competition pressure by turning it to our advantage and gaining the important 'competitive edge' by learning tips and techniques to channel the pressure for good. We shall learn to control anxiety and emotions with trigger points, EFT tapping, positive affirmations, visualisation, breathing, powerful self-analytical work-book analysis and a step by step approach to competition. There are ways of setting yourself up as best you can with tips and tricks for the reluctant competitor.

We shall look at competence v confidence. Learn to manage training and ultimately manage expectations to build up gently, improving your chances of doing well rather than trying to run before you can walk, which is more likely to lead to disappointment. Small, manageable goals are the key. Aim for the top of course, but don't be afraid to start at the bottom and work up. We shall work on accepting that some degree of pre-performance feelings are positive and the reason you put in hours of training is to be in a position where you can trust your skills in competition. As my trainer said to me once: "fail, learn, repeat, improve, win". Concise but nevertheless accurate.

AIMS AND AMBITIONS

Wanting to compete, feeling you are ready after a good ride or lesson is fantastic. The feeling stays with you and you go home or to the office ready to fill out the entry form for the show or competition. You are ready, you know you are and you are going to do this. Feeling super positive while you are at home or work in relative safety is one thing, but actually filling out the entry form is for many people where the problems start. The doubt and anxiety creep in and the entry form gets put in the bin or, more likely these days, the screen gets switched off without the online form being completed. You are keen and capable but your worries are stopping you from taking those first steps to enjoying some light-hearted competitive fun.

From the initial excitement of "right, I am going to do it this time" to actually completing and submitting the entry form and setting out on the day to compete is a big leap. When you don't make it, the spiral of upset starts. You may well feel like a failure because you didn't try, didn't go through with it and are inwardly upset that once again you let your anxiety win, letting the negative feelings grow. Before you know it, the  thought of doing anything where you are in the spotlight becomes a huge 'demon' and you side-step it whenever you can.

You are not alone, so make peace with yourself knowing that it's not just you. Then make yourself a promise to rectify this once and for all. A great many riders, who want to go to a show, jump a course or do dressage, TREC, working equitation, side saddle, showing or any other equine discipline you may care to think of feel the same way. In their hearts they really want to do it but their minds allow the 'wobbles', 'what ifs' and self-doubt to set in. The fear of the unknown takes hold and before they know it, they are stopped in their tracks, never daring to send the form off, let alone take part. You need to learn to turn the anguish in to a competitive 'fire' so that the excitement of the schedule or entry form stays with you beyond completing and posting it, to the day of the show and the competition itself.

Now, of course, not everyone wants to compete. We are often made to feel that we should or we are not worthy as horse owners and riders. I want to clear something up on this subject before I go any further. Despite being a keen competitor myself, I will not tolerate those horsey people who look down their noses at riders who are happy staying at home, schooling for their own personal joy, jumping for fun or hacking across beautiful countryside for pleasure. I will not tolerate the use of the word 'just' or 'only' in this context – "oh, she *just* rides at home", "oh, he *just* jumps at the yard", "oh she *just* hacks", "well, he *only* rides at home, don't you know".

The words "only" and "just" are very useful words to imply something derogatory or negative. I don't like to hear them used and I urge you to stop doing it right now if you are guilty of this self-deprecating crime or worse, use it to belittle others. You are not 'only' or 'just' anything, you ARE! My back goes up like an unhappy feral cat when I hear the term "just a happy hacker" used as a way of putting someone down for not competing. Let's be straight here, some of us are happy enjoying the countryside and not having any pressure or added hassle of going to shows, doing competitions and all it entails. Leave these people alone. Stop judging their choices.

Despite being a regular and keen competitor myself, I think hacking is the best. It's lovely and the best way to build up a relationship with your horsey companion, enjoying adventures in the countryside together. I have enjoyed hacking and distance riding for years and the challenges they present are numerous. So you could say I am a happy hacker. It's brilliant fun and you never know what is around the next corner. Far from being the choice of the less-accomplished rider, hacking will test your skills each time you set foot out in the big wide world. It is great for the fitness and mental well-being of the horse too. The arena is a sterile environment for the most part, but once you leave the gates of your yard or field, all kinds of interesting, unexpected and wonderful things can happen. Anyone belittling someone that 'just' hacks out is being very narrow-minded and frankly quite mean.

Let's for one minute think about the challenges these hacks can throw at us, from the refuse lorry, to a random dog or assorted wildlife suddenly appearing under a hedge. A constantly changing world presents obstacles and incidents which must be overcome immediately by the horse and rider in order to complete the ride, stay safe and get home again. For example, a recent hack as a break from writing this book was the usual mix of day-dreamy fun and unexpected situations. No word of a lie, my friend and I encountered deer on the tracks, lorries, cars, high speed (and not so high speed) lycra-clad cyclists on the roads and a helicopter landing next to a bridle way in a farmer's 'garden' almost on top of our heads. We are used to the first few encounters but a rather large helicopter coming down from the sky, right over our heads, bending the canopy of the trees and plonking itself down within one hundred metres of us was a shock and quite testing, not to mention noisy and breezy. What I am saying is, riders who hack have to think quickly, react quickly and take on the world some days so if you know anyone who uses the term 'happy hacker' in a less than friendly way, please ask them to be kinder with their appraisal and never do it yourself.

There may be other factors at play too, a rider may not have access to costly transport, lack funds for expensive entry fees or afford the 'right' showing attire required. Not to mention elderly horses that can no longer strut their stuff as they once did; people with stressful jobs who don't want to add competing at weekends to their already hectic schedules, or the uncompetitive people who are happy doing what they do with their horse already. So please, live and let live. We should all be united by our passion and love of horses, so whatever it is we do within the realms of equestrianism should be applauded and never belittled or mocked in any way. EVER.

I promise to stop going off at a tangent in a minute but this had to be addressed and I really hope that we as riders take a moment to understand that we are all different and it is a personal choice what we do, or indeed, not do with our beloved horses. It makes my blood boil to the point that despite writing a book on competing, I felt I had to mention this common slur. You will be pleased to know that now I have got that off my chest I will get back to the task in hand, helping you find your way to the showground and arena.

In some ways, I learned the hard way about competing. I learned to ride with un-wavering passion (and of course still learn now – we never stop) and quickly became aware of the wonders of rosettes. The desire to get a red ribbon or sash was so overwhelming I almost had palpitations just thinking about winning something (anything) and being presented with the coveted silky red frilly disc of wonder. Actually any colour would have done to start with, but I am a very competitive person by nature so the red or first prize was the most coveted. This is where I went wrong. I had a lovely little cob, surprisingly athletic, extremely clever and very spirited. I was having regular lessons from an instructor who was keen to point out that cobs can do good work. We soon found that mine was actually very good at the movements required for the entry levels of dressage and easily turned his hoof to a Prelim/Novice test while at home we were doing some work at Elementary for later on. He was probably unable to progress as far as some due to a previous issue, so I never pushed him to the limit, but we did work hard within capabilities and within an ethical evaluation of what was right for him.

He was well marked and moved nicely so would have done well in ridden showing too. Certainly at local and riding club level with his presence and good conformation he would hold his own when I took him showing in-hand so there was no reason not to try ridden classes. Jumping wasn't on the cards due to veterinary advice but flat work was good for him mentally and physically, not only something for him to think about but as a great aid for strengthening and keeping him flexible. At that time, all those years ago, although I wasn't particularly skilled as a rider to be doing anything too amazing, I was enjoying the learning curve and progression that this dear little chap, just 14 hands, was giving me week in week out.

After about a year of lessons, major improvement had been made and although I enjoyed hacking immensely, there was the inevitable talk of going to do some dressage tests or ridden shows to put all the hard work and hours of practice to the test. My instructor said those terrible words "you should go and do a ridden **show** or a dressage **test**". SHOW, TEST, oh my goodness. TEST, those terrible things you dread at school. TESTS. The mere word stopped me in my tracks and I wanted to be sick at the thought of doing a TEST. SHOW. What, why, oh no, help! Oh heck, performing in front of someone conjured up visions of great calamity, like being a shepherd in my junior school nativity play and needing the lavatory. TEST: being in a maths exam when you are rubbish at sums and forgot your calculator. That was it, terror had gripped me.

It wasn't until several years later that I worked with the feelings I had let snowball out of control, and learned how to change my perception to allow me to get past the barriers that my mind had, rather unhelpfully, put in place for me. I understand now that a simple word was the first issue because it conjured up dread from deep within my psyche. It didn't occur to me at the time while the terror gripped my throat and the nausea rose within me, that had he said "dressage," or casually, "a bit of dressage," it may have lessened the pressure. Although I would have been worried as I hadn't done it in public before, I still think I would have made less of a drama about it. Even if he had said, "let's go and try some dressage somewhere else in a proper arena," basically anything other than the word test, I think I would have reacted slightly differently. As it was, I had two things go through my head 1 – terror, 2 – I'm not good enough compared with the others (compared with others that I hadn't even seen ride, how on earth I came to that conclusion is still a mystery!).

What I now realise is that terror actually translated in my mind into: there will be calamity, I will be observed, I will be harshly judged, I will crumble, I will forget how to ride or do anything useful for the full four minutes, I will be laughed at, I will be in the spotlight, I will get the wrong canter lead and I will get the wrong trot diagonal. It was the same when he suggested ridden shows. The word "show" felt for me, the same as "test" and immediately made me think that I was not capable. Thoughts of wrong canter leads, wrong diagonals, being judged and not knowing where to go or what to do in the personal ridden show, this strange figure of eight that everyone in the world knew how to ride, except me (well, that's how it felt at the time). Not to mention what if I lose control and take out the judge, or what if the world suddenly opens up and I disappear into the pits of hell (probably unlikely but I have a powerful imagination). My 'doom mind-set' went in to overdrive.

Despite all the scenarios playing out non-stop in my head and managing to talk myself round most of them, believe it or not, the biggest one, the one that I couldn't get past and I am being very honest and open about this to prove how a simple thing can wreak havoc in your head was... wait for it... "I will get the wrong trot diagonal". More than anything else, this for me was the biggest fear in the world. I now understand this simple little thing in terms of mechanics and can feel every motion of the horse beneath me as my riding has improved. I even laughed about it years later with a dressage judge, who confirmed that "any judge would probably be more pleased that you came and had a go rather than mark you down provided the horse was in balance." I assumed that any little mistake (if indeed, I had even made it), would have been all defining. In my nightmares it was given out over the public address system: "you are on the wrong diagonal, please leave the arena, you are rubbish and should not be here." In my self-doubting world, everyone would have looked at me and laughed and told me I was useless. I didn't want to be useless. I wanted to be good.

I know I'm poking fun at myself now, but at the time this was a serious issue for me and I was unable to get past it. I desperately wanted to go and have a try but I cried with fear over the blessed trot diagonal and only rode dressage at home, on the correct damn diagonal and correct canter lead. It was so simple, the words "show" and "test", nearly stopped me getting out of the starting blocks which would have been a crying shame. I now enjoy showing, working equitation and dressage and have every hope of competing one of my home produced horses at Prix St Georges in the near future and, eventually, Grand Prix. This just proves that a 'scaredy cat' can turn in to a serious competitor with the right tools. That is the motivation for this book, to turn you into someone who can compete if you choose to and I hope my honesty and the fact that I can not only laugh about it but have got past it, will help and inspire you to carry on and get past your personal hurdles too.

My beloved pony is 26 now and retired in my field, thankfully in good health and I give thanks every day for whatever time he has left. I did do some in-hand showing with him as I felt I was capable of that (no pressure as I was beside him not on him), but I never did a ridden show or a dressage test with him and it breaks my heart to think back now to the wasted opportunities. He was more than capable and so was I, but the fear of competition and the self-doubt were so intense I always put it off and turned to distance riding where the pressure was off. I loved the distance riding and still do it now on my mare. We completed 1000 recorded miles together before he retired to more low-key local hacking. We have the most wonderful collection of rosettes and mileage awards. We had the most fun and I will be so proud of that achievement with my little intrepid warrior cob for the rest of my life.

However, in the back of my mind the dressage and showing challenge was always there and I have to admit to side-stepping it his entire ridden life. To this day I regret it and if I am honest, typing this my eyes are pricking with tears. I still, deep down have a big 'regret-shaped hole' in my heart because I let self-doubt and my fear of being judged overshadow my chance to get out there and shine and I felt I let us both down, which is really hard to get past even all these years later. Looking back we probably would have done really well but I blew it all out of proportion and in my head, a simple dressage test or ridden show became "riding at Olympic standard and being taken out by a firing squad" if I didn't do any good. That snowball of fear/self-doubt and me making up reasons not to even try meant it never happened.

Now, the chance is gone and I don't want that to happen to you so I have written this book in the hope you will be able to achieve your dreams. Don't do what I did. Cherish your horse, go to competitions, give it a go, have some fun, enjoy the moment. The fear of the competition is short-lived but the sadness of not trying will last a lifetime. Where there is sadness at not trying there should be memories of giving it a go, and who knows, maybe rosettes, sashes and even trophies.

I wish someone had given me this piece of advice back then as it would have changed my perspective and helped me realise that life is not a dress-rehearsal and to miss opportunities is extremely sad and so unnecessary.

If you had the chance now to look into the future and see your old horse retired in his field, knowing you cannot ride him because the years have taken their toll, would you be sad you never took the chance of competing, even just once, just trying? Would you look at him with sadness in your heart knowing you could have done it if you had the courage and self-belief? You know he would have got you round the course, done you proud in the show or owned it in the dressage. Now, he is old and the chance has passed. You will never forgive yourself for not giving it a go. You will never look at his ribbons with great affection and reminisce on  your achievements after he is dead and gone because there are none. Not one, and if you are like me, it will hurt. So get out there, try, be the best you can be, smile, enjoy the challenge and look back one day far from now with a warmth and affection that cannot be bought at a later date or on another horse. Look back in years to come and your heart will be full of pride because you tried. You were a team and you nailed it!

Although I missed my chance in some ways with this horse, I was later lucky enough to find myself in a professional equestrian environment for my work with AB Film Horses/AB Equitation as well as having two young horses of my own ready to take over from my dear old boy. Although having access to a horse was never a problem, my own mind was. I had to learn to re-train it, to approach things from a different angle; rational thought replacing terror and self-doubt with confidence, self-belief and a more laid back attitude to 'giving it a go'. I went to my first competition in the name of my old horse. I felt I wanted to do it for him and it gave me strength to see it through along with the valuable self-help techniques which I will share with you to help you get where you want to be.

Compete with your heart. Train your mind to support your heart. In all things. Always.

ANXIETY WITHIN SPORT

It would be difficult to find a sports person who doesn't in some way, react to competing. Anxiety, nerves, butterflies, stress, call it what you will, it is completely normal, borne from the desire to win, to do well, to shine and basically to show off yourself, and in this case, your horse, as best you can. In order to combat it, we must understand what it is in simple terms.

A medical definition of anxiety describes it as 'a state consisting of psychological and physical symptoms brought about by a sense of apprehension of a perceived threat which can differ according to the situation and the person'. Applying this to your competition anxiety may mean, for example, that the fear of being observed may worry you, while for some it could be that you experience more anxiety entering a national level event compared with a club or local level competition. Some people will be as nervous at club level as others are at a much higher level.

Psychologists generally differentiate between two types of anxiety: Trait anxiety relates to an aspect of personality in which nervousness is a personality trait, whereas State anxiety on the other hand refers to temporary feelings of anxiety in a particular situation. Therefore a person with an anxious personality may find many different everyday tasks stressful compared with someone who only gets nervous in extreme or uncertain situations such as competition.

There are no fast, easy fixes for anxiety, even for elite athletes with the best professional help in the world, but it can be effectively managed and dealt with so that it is not an issue for you. Clinical anxiety is different altogether and should be dealt with by a physician as it requires a proper treatment plan which may sometimes include medication. Assuming the anxiety you are experiencing is due to State anxiety there is no need for medication and with the right resources and practice, you can build up the skills to deal with your performance anxiety like a champion.

If you've ever watched top level sport of any kind you will have witnessed sports men and women performing under immense pressure. I am guessing you have at least watched, with thrill and joy, your chosen equine discipline being ridden by the Olympic Team or those at an equivalent high level. These incredible athletes exhibit nerves of steel and have the ability to put on their 'game face' and perform, being the best they can be for those moments when it counts. For most, this means managing the pressure, learning how to deal effectively with anxiety. This could range from a simple heightened state to debilitating emotional and physical upset that would surely ruin their game, if not leave them unable to compete at all.

Nerves and anxiety levels vary from person to person but more often than not, individuals wanting to perform to their best ability will feel something before being 'on show'. Professionals can enlist the help of sports psychologists who mentor them and teach them how to prepare mentally and perform in competition. However, we every-day riders generally don't have those resources. This is where this book steps in, to allow you to be your own coach, set your own goals and learn some of the techniques that the higher level sports people may use. After all, we all know the horse needs to be trained but rarely consider people do too.

Ok, so you could just go ahead and expect to be nervous before a competition. This may sound crazy but for some people, this is all there is to it. They accept they will be nervous and go ahead and do it anyway. I think we all like the idea of completely banishing our nerves but in practice, it's unrealistic to expect to feel nothing, we need to feel some excitement in order to perform. The key is to learn to control and work with anxiety. It isn't necessarily harmful unless it is absolutely crippling in which case we must learn to address it and work with it. For many competitors, an adrenaline rush which is triggered by anxiety can actually be beneficial on a physiological level. Sports psychologists may teach their clients to come to terms with their anxiety and use it for good.

It's more helpful to accept that you're probably always going to feel some level of nervousness before an event and that it doesn't have to stop you from doing what you need to do. You have to learn to control it to work with it. It is important to understand that even if the final outcome is out of your hands, there are some things you *can* control in the moment and this is where good training and preparation come in. Entering a competition knowing you have done all you can at home should bring courage and relief because you are armed with the skill to succeed. Training, whether mentally or physically is the thing we can manage and this helps stack the odds in our favour.

DISCIPLINES

For the purposes of the book and to keep it to just the one manageable volume, I will generally refer to the disciplines of dressage, showing and jumping. I will occasionally refer to other sports such as TREC, working equitation etc, but whatever discipline you ride in, you can use the guides and ideas here by tailoring them to your exact needs in your chosen equine sport. I am sure you can translate the advice to whatever you do with your horse: barrel racing, western, western dressage, trail, mounted horse agility, polo, horse ball, *voltige* (vaulting), reining, *doma vaquera*, *doma clásica* , carriage driving, endurance, cross country, jump cross, in-hand showing, trick riding, liberty, mounted games, adult gymkhana, whatever it is.

This is a book for anyone who rides a horse, in any discipline, anywhere in the world. It is a strategy for anyone who doesn't compete but wants to start, or for those who compete occasionally but want to up their game and try bigger challenges without the nerves taking over. This book is a tool, something to get you going and learn how to break down your fears and by taking smaller, manageable steps to become brave enough to compete as much as you want to, wherever you want to, in whatever you want to as well as enjoying it along the way. This is about making your mind and body work for you, not against you. I am going to use dressage, showing and jumping as examples but if you think about your equine sport, you can easily translate the points/advice and strategies to match your needs.

Dressage

Dressage, lovingly referred to by some as 'stressage', should be called 'accurately riding patterns to markers for fun' because it is exactly that when you put it in perspective. It is simply a way of teaching a horse in a controlled way through the 'scales of training' to learn to carry himself correctly and use his body to perform certain movements. Originating from the military it is just a form of training. Simplified, it is walk,

trot, canter and then later, more advanced variations of those things. It is the culmination of all your hard work and a chance to show off your horse and your riding, whatever level you are at. The rewards are great, especially when you take a young horse from his first Intro and start to climb the ranks as he grows up and learns more skills. His training and capability will progress from a wobbly walk and trot to getting better impulsion and all four feet in the right place as he starts to understand what you are asking. Further on, your first laterals or feeling his power when riding his first few steps of *Passage* will be thrilling. For the older or established horse, it is great fun as your scores improve at the chosen levels, you feel him relax in his work and can ride a beautiful straight centre line in walk, or at the other end of the scale perhaps perform the canter pirouette or flying changes.

For the veteran horse it is a way to keep him fit and supple, hopefully prolonging his working life, even if it means downgrading from where he would compete in his prime to be kinder and more thoughtful towards him. There is no shame in asking him to do less strenuous movements to take into account his physicality (this is relevant for a young horse too, steady progression is the key). For the horses that can't climb the ranks or the riders who don't want to, dressage can still be enjoyed at any level. There is no shame about finding where you are comfortable and staying there if that is what you want to do. Don't be afraid to try though.

Most good horses, if trained correctly can achieve Elementary or possibly Medium level but again, whichever level you choose is fine. Don't let me define your goals. My friend had a beautiful horse, they stayed at Intro level forever, they were happy doing walk and trot tests and had a great deal of fun. The key is that they were happy. Always make sure you are happy in your riding. It is, after all, the whole point of having a horse. Whatever you decide is right, do it for you. Always set your own benchmark and don't be led into riding someone else's dream or getting drawn in to situations because of peer pressure or other factors.

Another thing I have learned (and this is the important part), is that dressage judges do not carry firearms (or use them). They are armed only with a pen and (most of them) a smile! They know what it's like to be wonky up the centre line, knock over the flowerpot at E, or have a horse that stops for a poo at F. They know how it feels to forget the test half way round, not to mention suddenly failing to know which way is right and which is left. Guess what? Judges in any discipline are actually human. Yes, I know this is a shock, but they are only judges because they have ridden the path you are on and understand where you are at. They know what it's like when it goes well and they know what it feels like when it goes wrong. What's more, although we pay to enter the competition itself, the Judges are usually either getting enough money for travel and expenses or more likely at local events, they are giving up their time, for free, so the last thing they want to do is upset anyone or appear mean. Obviously they have to be impartial and professional so tend to avoid lengthy chats with competitors as they enter the arena, which may come across as a bit scary, but they definitely appreciate a smiling rider and someone giving it a damn good go and being sportsmanlike whatever the outcome.

I have found that it mostly goes right once you get down to business, no matter if you are riding at Intro or higher. Go up the centre line like you own it. As with any show, your first impressions are going to set you up well, take a deep breath and 'enter at A' like a pro. If it does start to go a little off course, don't worry. We all make mistakes. If the bell goes, they will be able to correct you and you can go on from there. Don't let one mistake de-rail you, but if it does, accept it as 'one of those days' and try again in the future or ride another test later that day if you can. Just because it went wrong once, does not mean it will mess up every time. The judge, writer and stewards will be there for you as much as they can in a scheduled environment. From my experience, it will more than likely go right, but if not, there is no tannoy announcement to shame you. Just a bell. Nobody loudly shouts out a list of your mistakes for all to hear. The judge or steward may ring the bell to notify you of an error (sometime this is a car hooter) and may speak to you to advise the error, but nobody will do it in a nasty way. One thing is for sure, whatever happens, they have been there and want you to keep going. Hold your head up high, re-ride the error, give it another go and live to fight another day.

Guess what else? If it goes right, which is more likely, they will still encourage you to come back another day to see if you can beat your previous score. They are actually not there to belittle you but to do what you have asked them to do in a fair and honest way: judge you. This judgement is not a mean and soul-destroying event, it is merely one person, observing one horse and rider at one moment in time. It is not all-defining and if you did the same test tomorrow, with the same judge, on the same horse, it may go differently. As a competitor, we have to accept that is a fact and keep at it and keep smiling. At the end, take your sheet and you can quietly evaluate the comments and marks and use them to build for the future.

Another thing to remember: if a competitor on a former advanced-level horse is doing really well at a lower level than where you may have expected to see them, don't automatically assume they are a 'pot-hunter'. Have you ever thought that maybe you don't know the full story? Could it be the rider is learning the ropes like you, but just lucky enough to have a highly-schooled horse with which to do so? Maybe they are scared stiff as well, so want to start at the bottom and work up. Maybe the horse carries an old injury that means he has all the 'buttons' but it would be unfair on him to press them.

From another stand point, if someone from your group or your yard just got 50% because it didn't go to plan today, beyond supporting each other, something in my experience the horsey community can be extremely poor at, it really shouldn't matter to you as it's not your story. They may actually be very pleased to have got round at that level if it is new to them, so 50% may be a huge achievement. Or it may be true that it didn't go to plan and they had a bad day. Either way, that's their reality, not yours. For your own sanity, only ever consider your own score and your own progression. First or top few placings are lovely but be realistic and when they happen, enjoy it, when they don't, just look at your result and see what you can do to improve for next time.

Dressage, like so many equine disciplines is all about YOU and YOUR horse, there are so many factors at play that you will never justify them all. For example, a young or inexperienced horse may make some errors where as an older or experienced horse may be brilliant and get a fantastic score beating you because he knows his job and/or was very well ridden. However, don't make the mistake of thinking "I don't know why they are in my class, they shouldn't have been there". Everyone can do whatever class they want to as long as it is within the rules of that particular competition. I have heard people say this type of thing so many times and it is petty, undignified and not very kind. Yes, ok, some people are 'pot hunters'. They stick at a level because they know they can do well or win every time and yes, of course, it does annoy us if we are honest, but really and truly, is it actually winning? It may be *placing highly* but winning is about progression and dedication shining through long term, pushing to compete alongside the best you can find to go up against as well as striving to beat your personal best. Really, if you boil it down, are they just kidding themselves? They are not being very fair but such is life and you aren't going to change them by moaning about them (or to them) so only concentrate on your horse, your riding and your score.

Some competitors, if they keep winning but don't want to or cannot move up a level, to be more gracious to others, may compete *Hors Concours* (HC) where the score is recorded but not included in the final line up. Dressage is the art of training the horse to be manoeuvrable, supple, educated, relaxed, obedient to the aids and ultimately a pleasure to ride. Over time he will improve his way of going, moving with cadence and self-carriage while in turn, improving his scores. The pattern is only there as a benchmark, something to form a level playing field for all competitors to be judged in the form of sport. Whether another rider is competing a horse that should in terms of its training, be way further up the levels or way further down from where you are, shouldn't matter one bit to you. The score on the day is the competition, it's what you signed up for by entering, but it is not the be all and end all. It is your score that matters.

The be all and end all is the improvement you and your horse are making, the progression over time which you can look back on with pride. Every one percent is a bonus. Keep this in your mind and watch your scores improve, see how the comments change and find joy in anything positive. There will always be days when it doesn't go so well. Don't worry, don't hold on to that. Just keep your sense of humour and come back another day to have a go again. Improvement comes from perseverance and when you get your first 7, 8, or even the odd 9 on a test sheet, you will be over the moon. If you get a 10, frame the test sheet!

The other thing we need to understand about dressage is that mostly, unless it is a big prestigious event or someone has the flashiest horse and everyone wants a peek, hardly anyone watches for very long. The time slots work well as the people hanging around are usually competing before and after you, so you will find they are really only interested in their own performance. Try to think in terms of your scores and your journey/personal best, not anyone else's.

My other advice is start at the beginning. No matter what your horse is capable of, if doing an entry level or Intro test makes you feel more in control than a higher level, then go for it. You will be able to get a few competitions under your belt before you move up, if indeed you want to. Once you feel more comfortable getting out there competing then you can go up the levels as you wish. The sky is the limit. I reiterate, by entering the class we are asking these judges to critique and score us and so they are commenting on what they see without any background knowledge of you or your horse. Most are very kind with their comments and despite the limited amount of time available to have it written down, will usually give encouragement as well as pointers on how to improve. Humans tend to dwell on the negatives but we need to stop this. Look at the sheet as a whole, look at the positives, then look at the negatives. Try to see them as pointers, see these comments as the valuable ones. After all, these are the things the judge thinks you can work on and improve. A smart competitor will really take the 'needs to improve' comments on board and work hard to make these things better rather than get upset about them.

Once you have seen the balance of the comments you should have a decent idea of what to do in your next training sessions as well as have an understanding of what can score you well and what you can do to improve. If you are designing a floorplan for a musical test, for example, it can really help to know what to put in there to make you look fabulous. Again, the judges are just scoring that move at that moment. Accept that although it is a learned opinion, it is after all just an opinion so try and see the validity of it rather than being upset and screwing the sheet up in a temper if it didn't read exactly as you thought it would. An example of this is a musical test I did at Novice, it was a big piece of music and some judges loved it and others weren't so keen! I won and 'lost' with the same test. A few people asked why I kept doing it as I was placed high in the national league at that time and the risk of the judge not liking it was going to cost me dearly in points. My horse was going really well and I was consistently getting good marks for the riding but the 'creative (interpretive) elements were just not to everyone's liking. We affectionately called it the "Marmite Test" as I never knew which way the scores would go. The reason I kept riding it is because I absolutely loved it! I loved the floor-plan, I loved the music and I wasn't going to give it up as it made me happy doing it which to me was the most important thing of all. I still use the test to warm up sometimes when schooling at home. It still makes me smile and my horse still knows the music which also makes me smile as he clearly enjoys riding it too. Go with your heart, never let anyone put you off.

Also, with dressage, unless you are competing at a level where a commander is not allowed, why add pressure by not having someone call your test? Of course it is good practice and makes sense to learn the test inside out, but you will feel a whole lot more confident knowing that if you do get out there and have a lapse in concentration, someone will be there calling it for you as back up, giving you that extra peace of mind.

A few words of caution: do make sure the commander a) knows your test and understands it so they can glance up as they call it to check you are both still on course, b) knows they will have to shout VERY loudly for you to hear them, c) have practised at home calling for you so they know how far ahead you like it to be read out and they don't drag behind or get too far in front of the movement you are doing, d) read it clearly as when you are cantering along with the wind in your ears and the horse is breathing, C, E, D, G and B can sound very similar, so remind the commander to really exaggerate and annunciate clearly.

The last thing they want to do is make a mistake causing you to go wrong, so the more you can practise together, the better. On the whole mistakes can be avoided with some practise and planning! Many of us try to rush ourselves in competition. The smart competitors are the ones that see it as a long game and build up the levels slowly and methodically. The fact that you are putting measures in place to avoid over-facing yourself will pay off in terms of reducing the nerves and, when things go well, it will significantly help increase your feelings of confidence and make you want to go back another day rather than dread it to the point of tears or not entering.

Showing

Showing, be it ridden or in-hand, is a few minutes' display, a small fragment of time in which the rider or handler must do their best to 'show off,' giving the judge a picture of what the horse is capable of, how well schooled and how elegantly he moves. The judges and stewards are again, probably there for free, giving up their time to stand in the arena in all weathers and watch you go round. We must  never forget that we are putting ourselves out there to be judged so judged we will be! As with all sport, there are things we can control (our preparation and training) and things we cannot (weather, other competitors, noises etc). For example, if the ring is set up next to the generator powering the snack wagon, you may well have a spook (having had a beautiful display of unexpected 'airs above the ground' when someone switched on the generator by the ringside when my young horse was next to it) but it is what it is. We have to accept that the show ground by its very nature will have all kinds of noises and things going on and, although it is naturally daunting for the newcomer, there are ways of easing yourself in gently rather than making your first time out Horse of the Year Show or the equivalent.

Local shows will hopefully be less full on, while the county shows, nationals and bigger venues are something to work towards, should you wish to, once you have established confidence at the smaller events. Most shows will have a lot of coming and going, loud PA systems (don't park underneath the speaker but do park where you can hear it or see your ring so you don't miss your class) and potentially other livestock at the county events. Both can be busy affairs and everyone who has ever done a show will no doubt have a tale of glory and a tale of something that didn't go to plan. While the latter may not have been much fun at the time, down the line the episode will fade to become a good tale to tell and something to smile about. Remember, nothing is worth dwelling on or it will just get to you and start to eat away at your nerves. We ride for fun and it is wise to remember that. I have done large shows at huge chaotic, noisy showgrounds and of course, numerous local shows and I have to say, if an alien came down, I am sure he would wonder why riders think that going in amongst all of the chaos is the best way to show off a horse.

Let's face it, it can be a little bit full on sometimes, but what we need to remember is 1) everyone who is there is facing the same landscape as you, 2) horses that are less than perfect because of the external factors will only learn to be show-perfect if they keep attending, 3) practise makes perfect. Putting a horse in the field does not train him to learn and understand the job we want him to do, so keep going to as many shows and events as necessary to teach the horse what is expected of him. He will soon learn the ropes, understand the part he has to play and yield. Horses are smart enough to work out that if their day starts with bathing and plaiting it probably means they are going somewhere and will learn that once they have done their 'job', they're back on the box with a hay net and homeward bound. Case in point of this is to see a seasoned pro, standing tied to the box, resting one leg, calmly waiting for his moment rather than fidgeting and determinedly trying to rub his plaits out, because he has seen it a 'million' times and knows that he does his performance and then gets left in peace to travel home and eat.

Showing should be a fun day out and if we handle it in the right way and approach it sensibly it can be. Start small and work up to bigger events. There is no shame in doing a tack and turnout type class where there is minimal ring-craft required beyond a gleaming horse, super smart rider and very clean tack, before you enter a class that does require a personal show and will no doubt be more daunting in the early days. If you do go in to a class where walk, trot and canter is desired, you can opt out of canter but will of course lose marks and placings by doing so. If you are not ready to canter in public, I would advise you enter a class where it is walk/trot only, these are usually marked as such on the schedule. In any event, plan your appearances cleverly, don't gallop before you can trot, as it were, and you will be fine.

Going to clinics or workshops is a good idea if you can, even if it is without your horse the first time. You can watch others from the floor, then once you have observed and feel ready to progress to taking your horse, go for it. Clinics, workshops or master classes are a great way to improve without the pressure of an actual show. I have done these myself and the knowledge you can glean from a top judge or world class competitor is immeasurable. Unlike in the arena or ring at an actual event, you can ask questions, discuss issues or elements and get valid feedback without being disqualified or losing marks. This takes away the pressure and helps you build up confidence and self-belief. Whatever your chosen field, do try to do at least the odd clinic if you can.

I did a wonderful showing clinic with a former Horse of the Year Show judge and it was not only good for us riding and learning how to do a ridden show that the judge would *want* to see, but she also advised each person individually from grass roots to higher levels of competition. She said whatever the level, keep it reasonably short whilst demonstrating the required elements and always keep it manageable, which is probably music to most of our ears. She explained that although she, like any judge, wants to see you show your horse off, she would never want you to feel rushed or pressured. You must be realistic about timing. A relatively short, well-ridden, well-thought-out show, is perfectly sufficient as long as it demonstrates the required gaits for the level of show you have entered. She went on to say that over-complicating things when you start out is more likely to worry you and put you off so do a simple, effective show which you can cope with mentally and will be great for showing off the paces of your horse.

This is great news for most, as it means that you have time to show your horse off without going round and round for ages which can, let's face it, annoy the other competitors and the judge may well switch off slightly. Make a show that has impact, is neat, looks effortless, plays to your strengths and makes the judge think "wow, that was nice" so that they remember you and place you well.

Although the horse is the one in the spotlight in terms of his way of going, don't forget overall presentation is important and the rider needs to be pristinely turned out and super-smart. Being smart doesn't mean having ridiculously expensive gear, but ensuring what you do wear is suitable for your class. It should be clean, tidy, fit well, the colour scheme work well with your horse and be appropriate for the type of show you are doing. If you are in doubt, muted tones are generally acceptable with bright colours to be avoided and no flags (check the rules) on your jacket or numnah. Military dress may be worn in some instances. In foreign breed classes, check the rules or with the organiser to see if they are allowing traditional dress, English attire or either. In all cases, check what you can in advance.

Do not try a new bit, new saddle, new pair of riding boots or indeed a new anything on the day. If you or the horse doesn't get on with something you haven't at least tried on and ridden in, you are asking for trouble. Go with what you know and what works. The time for new bits, new boots and new tack is at home, not when you need everything to be 'comfortable' and familiar. As long as everything is clean, you can try your new things another day. If you are unsure what to wear, maybe phone the organiser or take several options with you on the day if you have them (or can borrow some variations). Do your homework, look online, talk to other people who have ridden recently in that type of class. Better still, go and watch the level and type of class you want to compete in. What are the majority of competitors wearing, doing and how are they showing themselves off? Social media groups can be great for this too, although if you ask a simple question online, you rarely get a simple answer or a consistent one for that matter. However you proceed, knowledge is power, so use it.

The following diagram of a simple, ridden, English show is generally suitable to show off your horse and not be too long or too short for most events. Higher level shows or specific breed or type shows may mean you will need to change your show to suit, but YouTube is great for this, as is going to watch a few classes. Very occasionally, a judge may request a specific set of movements they want to see. I have never experienced this at local level, except in a class where you have a jump (e.g. working hunter) but occasionally at county or national this may be the case. Definitely expect it in a driving class if you are a carriage driver at county level as in my experience they often throw you a curve-ball and ask for a specific set of movements (depending on the type of class you enter).

For those unfamiliar with a ridden show, below are some tips for guidance. However, do check the exact requirements of the class you are entering in advance:

- As you approach the ring, and certainly once you are in, it's game time, so no slouching and ride properly, let all your good training shine through. Now is not the time to panic or try something new.
- Breathe and smile!
- You will be invited in to the ring by the steward who will direct you to start walking in a clockwise direction. Don't fiddle and flap, ride quietly and effectively to the best of your ability.
- In most classes you will walk, trot and canter on both reins with the steward directing you where to go. If you are unsure and don't want to go first, let a couple of competitors in before you so you can take their lead and follow until you are more sure of yourself.
- The Judge will invite the competitors to line up in the ring once he or she has seen you go round as a group. This can be in a provisional order of favourites or, sometimes, no particular order at all. Don't worry, just do as you are told and stay calm. If you have been pulled in first you will

have to perform your personal show first. Stick to what you have practised at home.

- In the line-up, while waiting for the others to do their show, don't switch off. Sit up straight (but relaxed) and silent. Talking during someone else's performance is rude. If you are not first to go, use this chance to watch other competitors' shows. It is unwise to change your show last minute because others are doing something different, but watch how they make use of the space in the ring etc. This is how you learn. However, once in the ring, stick to your own plan unless you are super confident you can cope and have the skills required to throw in a sudden change.
- When riding your personal show, take into account the position of the judge, anything scary at ringside where you may need more leg, the ground conditions under hoof and be considerate to the other competitors by not cutting across or too near them.
- Make sure you are ready when the steward calls you out of line. Don't sit there looking bored or half asleep. You want your horse to be relaxed but also ready to walk over to the judge looking his best, not tripping over and dilly dallying with you frantically gathering your reins.
- When you get to the judge, always smile and say good morning (afternoon/evening as appropriate). Make your horse stand square. He needs to be alert and attentive; quiet but not fidgeting, nor so relaxed he rests one leg.
- The judge may ask a few questions regarding your horse's name, age, breed or any number of things so be prepared to answer politely. There is no need to use 1000 words when 10 will do as in this situation the judge wants answers but not a discussion. When the judge asks you to start your show you should walk away in a straight line. It is not polite to rush off from the judge in a cloud of dust, so always walk first.
- Your show should be consistent, showing control, quality of paces, fluent transitions and a clear difference between the paces you are riding as well as a square halt start and finish.
- To finish your personal show, halt in front of the judge or to one side where they can see you clearly (i.e. not miles away but don't run the judge over either!). After the halt, salute with a nod of the head (gentlemen may tip their hat if there is no chin strap or gesture as much by bowing the head and tipping the peak slightly). This is a gesture to thank the judge for his or her time watching you and must not be forgotten.
- Good use of the ring, understanding the lie of the land and the ground conditions are important but ring craft will come from practice so can be worked on over time.

- The judge will know that some competitors are more experienced than others so don't let this worry you too much. Everyone has to start somewhere but having said this, you will do better if your horse is behaving.
- After your salute, make your way back to the line-up in walk. Return to your original place and always go back to the line from behind, never cut across or in front of anyone else.

An example show

English ridden and probably most shows will include walk, trot and canter on both reins plus a gallop. An example of an individual show is as follows:
- Walk away from the judge in a straight line
- Trot a large half circle before changing the diagonal across the centre.
- Canter as you continue the figure of eight. If you established the correct bend you should get the correct leg. Canter a large half circle and return to trot to cross the diagonal.
- Repeat on the other rein but do not change the diagonal this time.
- Gallop on at a safe distance from the line up (if required) before returning to a balanced canter.
- Come smoothly back to trot and walk before halting beside or near the judge.
- Enjoy your show but keep it short by being as precise as you can.
- A simple but effective ridden show is pictured below.

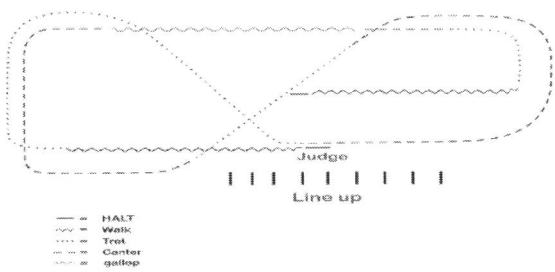

EASY IDEAS
TO OVERCOME PRESSURE

A great tip for the reluctant competitor is to go slightly outside your area if you are worried about being watched by people you know. It's worth going incognito, albeit perhaps with a trusted friend. Taking someone with you is a really good plan. You will appreciate the moral support and the extra pair of hands, as well as someone to hold the horse or go and collect your number and sign you in with the Secretary while you are tacking up or getting your outfit on. Some people will prefer to be on familiar ground surrounded by people they know but, for many, that actually adds to the pressure. You need to work out which scenario worries you the most and plan from there. I have found there can be far less pressure if you travel a little further rather than going to the local place where all the other horsey people you know will be.

Whether dressage, jumping, carriage driving, eventing, cross country, showing or whatever you are competing at it could be well worth getting up that little bit earlier to go off slightly further afield. It doesn't have to be miles, just a different area from that usually frequented by the majority of people from your immediate area and peer group. People are notorious creatures of habit so you would be amazed that by travelling in the opposite direction from where you normally associate the horsey events in your area you won't know a soul.

On the other hand, if you go a few times, you will undoubtedly make some new friends and then not feel pressured anyway which is ironic as you were avoiding the masses originally. This worked for me and it helped in the early days when I was anxious about what to do and unsure of myself. Personally, the stress caused by people I know can really add to the butterflies on the day, so by removing that factor I can reduce my anxiety by quite some measure. I realise this is not an option for some people if they have no transport but maybe ask to borrow a friend's box or do a lift share with one other person. Alternatively, it may be worth saving up as many self-drive hire companies offer a day deal on a trailer or a small horsebox.

I know a lot of people feel that you should push as hard as you can in competition, but don't worry about the opinion of others and just do what is right for you. For example, just because you are happy jumping a certain height at home, why not do a smaller course the first few times? This way, you will feel confident that you and your horse are more than capable and this will ease the pressure considerably. You can always do the bigger course next time or, if the first round goes well and you and your horse are feeling good, you can probably enter another class on the day or go for a clear round at the next height. Give your horse a chance to familiarise himself with the jumps and the arena or course before entering your actual class. There is no great shame in doing this, you can get your horse relaxed and if things go well you will know that you could have done a higher level but can go home happy and attack it again the following week or next time you are out.

As with the dressage and showing, play to your strengths. If you know your horse is great cross-country through water, pick a venue where you have this question and can enjoy excelling at it. Similarly, if you know your horse isn't great with water, pick a course with none or a smaller element. You can work your way up to the bigger water-jump when you have perfected it at home. Also, many cross-country venues do allow you to hire the facilities when they have no competitions which is the best way to familiarise yourself with the course. It is the same for show jumping venues which often have the facilities up for hire during the week, so get down there, put up the most horrible fillers and combinations you can find so that when you go back 'for real' you have seen the worst they have to throw at you and know you can do it.

Some instructors will go with you to a venue for a lesson. If not, enquire about an in-house trainer or go with a friend who can video you or help you. Video is a great way of looking at your own training, position, striding, contact and all the subtle things needed to succeed. You can show it to your instructor who can give you more  pointers and things to work on to improve and help with your overall confidence. Don't forget, whatever your competition favourite, try to school your horse in other disciplines for a well-rounded happy life. Imagine how you would feel if you only went round in circles or only jumped. Excel at something and stick with it but try to mix it up a little for your own sanity and more so for that of your lovely horse.

ONLINE COMPETITIONS

We will look at the pros and cons of social media next. I will leave you to decide how you handle it but, on a big plus note, I have had a great experience with and highly recommend online dressage. I have not only competed online but also sponsored a series of 'confidence classes' to encourage others to give it a go. My website **www.confident-rider.co.uk** and the **Confident Rider (@confidentriderhuo**) Facebook page have details. As does my Facebook group **Horse Riders: Nervous/anxious/Lost Confidenc**e (see link at the back of this book). We have tried to be inclusive and introduced all kinds of classes suitable for anyone to join in, including a walk only dressage in addition to the usual Intro, Prelim, Novice etc. A hacking challenge with mileage rosettes as well as some showing classes which I hope will help boost the rider in terms of having a go and realising they are good enough to take part.

We are based in the UK but accept entries from riders anywhere in the world which makes an exciting mix of riders and horses. Given my continuing desire to encourage anxious riders, my classes are of course open to anyone but particularly for those who are lacking confidence or may not usually want to compete. I feel the online route can be a good starting point as there is less pressure than a big day out where you have to actually go somewhere, not to mention it is less time consuming and less costly! The classes have been very well received and many of the riders have emailed me to thank us (me and the organisers) for "giving them a chance". One lady messaged and said that she would "never have dared enter a normal class" but (the restriction had) "given her the confidence to try." Now she realises she can do it and "intends to do more classes in the future," which is brilliant.

Entering these or similar types of online classes is a great way of trying different tests, putting your toe in the water but still being appraised by judges who are kind and constructive with their comments. Not only does it give you confidence to try and get some feedback, you receive your test sheet in the post and, if you are placed in the top ten, a rosette. All competitors get some sweets in the envelope with their test sheet too, so nobody is left out of a reward for their efforts. Sometimes there are fun classes such as any tack (i.e. not British Dressage legal), fancy dress

or pairs, as well as Prix Caprilli which are classes which involve poles and jumps. I urge you to think about online competitions if you think you can't currently face competing at a venue but can muster the courage to do it online to get you started. However, it can be addictive and great fun so who knows, you may get a taste for the scary world of dressage and keep doing more and more tests!

Providing you can set up an 'arena' with markers (upturned plant pots painted with letters and poles on the ground are sufficient), then you can compete. No transport needed. There are numerous gadgets available to film you, or ask a willing friend to video you with a camera or smart phone. The classes run from entry or Intro and fun classes to the more serious higher levels, it is brilliant fun and the temptation to be an online competitor rather than go out is certainly there and if that is the case, don't knock it. As well as dressage, I know there have been various online shows, working equitation, jumping and all sorts available, especially recently as the popularity of online events grows. There are competitions to suit everyone and it's just brilliant. Online showing could be a great starting point for the reluctant competitor to dress up smartly, video themselves riding and submit to being judged. Some online shows are even done with a photograph. A great way of checking you are wearing the right outfit/tack and the feedback will no doubt help your self-esteem and play a small part in your battle against competition anxiety. After all, you are being judged but not in the full-on real world. It is a good stepping stone to getting out there and strutting your stuff in public.

For any doubters, or 'moaners' who doubt the validity of this, let's just say that any form of organised competition is valid providing it is done fairly and professionally. As I always say, if you go up the centre line for a judge you are competing. Don't put yourself down and certainly don't rule out this type of online competition in any discipline to get your confidence going and get you started. Who knows, you may actually get hooked.

SOCIAL MEDIA PRESSURE

Let's for one moment look at the other people you are exposed to on social media or at the yard. Their actions should not matter to you, but invariably we are affected by the opinions of others resulting in (unintentional) pressure from our peers and even our friends. We naturally compare ourselves. Social media has its place for building people up but it can also bring us crashing down. Constantly being exposed to friends posting pictures of huge cross country fences or jumping the wings, winning dressage competitions, showing a horse so covered in rosettes you cannot see his head sets a benchmark. It can give the impression that unless we can beat or equal their triumphs we are unworthy. Those pictures of success are great for that person but they can sometimes increase our feelings of inadequacy and start the negative cycle of self-doubt. Although we are of course pleased for them, and wish them nothing but luck in their horsey pursuits, these constant comparisons, over time, can have a detrimental effect on our mental well-being.

We may not even realise how much we are affected and how much we compare ourselves with others, including those we 'follow' or are 'friends' with on social media. Ask yourself, in reality, how many of these people do you *actually* know and how many do you see regularly? How many are *real* friends and how many are people you hardly know and possibly have never met? You may be soaking up their successes like a sponge. You may start to feel less successful, less capable and just plain old down in the dumps. It is a big price to pay if you are pitting yourself against people you don't really know and are just 'following.' Constantly looking at someone's profile is ok but not to the detriment of your self-esteem. Don't let this happen, don't let it get control of you so that you start doubting your self-worth.

I'm not a huge fan of social media as I think it can be a spotlight for idiots as well as give false information and false hope. That may be because I, like many my age, just don't really 'get it' to the extent that it involves posting or checking it relentlessly in the form of habit. I am sure my niece and nephew would disagree and tell me off for not embracing this exciting new element of worldwide 'culture.' My retort, whilst rolling my eyes, is that I am doing what I feel comfortable with so that it remains enjoyable and productive. That said, I do have a confident rider page on Facebook and post to Instagram when I have something good to share rather than bombarding it with rubbish every five minutes. If I am posting anything, I want it to be worth something and have a valid reason behind it. I feel that there is enough pressure comparing yourself with your actual friends, let alone all these others. Look at it this way: in the 'old days' (yes, I'm over the age of 45!) we would aspire to be like people we looked up to, our heroes, probably professional riders on TV. We would compare ourselves with those horse riders immediately around us who were doing well but, in most cases, this was a handful of people in the local area. Now we log on to social media and unwittingly compare ourselves with hundreds if not thousands of people all doing what appear to be amazing things, all the time, on wonderful horses. They seem to be winning enough rosettes to wallpaper their lounge and their successes are being put on display every minute of the day.

I'm not saying for one minute that social media is all bad, but take everything with a pinch of salt. Remember that people only tend to put their horsey triumphs on their pages and a photo is a millisecond in time. It isn't necessarily the before and after or, in fact, even the truth in some cases. Triumph at competition is great but don't let it define you, especially if it's someone else's glory. Set your own goals with your horse, allow others to inspire you but not define you. Enjoy the time you spend online, it can be great fun and informative, but don't lose track of reality and most importantly, don't let other peoples 'stuff' affect you in a negative way. Easier said than done I know. As a physical exercise, from this very minute, try to limit how often you check these pages, live your life in the now, in the real world, in YOUR reality. Never let these 'posts full of glory' take hold of you and get inside your mind, especially if you are feeling unsure or anxious about your capability as a competitor or rider. For an eye-opening exercise, make a note in the course of an evening or throughout a 24-hour period of how often you are scrolling through social media. Is it too often and are you living your life in a 'fake' world in which everyone appears to have perfect lives/horses? By all means enjoy it but be aware and control it, don't let it dictate and control you.

THE COMPETENCE/CONFIDENCE EQUATION

In order to understand our mentality or mind-set we must look at it in greater detail. However, we must also look at the physical and practical reasons behind the mentality which are often to do with capability. I refer to this as the competence/confidence equation which we will explore next, as well as looking at ways to overcome the deficit if, indeed, there is one.

Competence v Confidence – the ultimate balance!

We have looked at positives and the last things you expect in a self-help book are negatives but honesty is important so at this point I will promise you a few things: there is no magic cure; there is no special head collar or contraption to make your horse 100% perfect; nobody can cure your fear without you taking responsibility for it and working to resolve the issues. You have to a) want a way forward b) be prepared to work at achieving your goals and c) realise there will be ups and downs along the way. Therefore, it is of paramount importance to discover whether the 'what if' fear is manifesting itself because you don't have the skills to deal with the problem in the first place, or if it is down to over-thinking the worst case scenario when in actual fact you are a competent rider and have just found yourself bogged down in gloom.

Recognising the reason can be quite difficult but despite how it may feel it is actually *positive* and a huge step towards dealing with the issue currently affecting your mind-set and your riding. This is where self-analysis through the following workbook will help. The lists dig deep and reveal the true answers so you can start to build your positive mind-set and get that entry form completed and sent off. However, in order to progress if there is a skill deficit causing your anxiety, we must address the competence/confidence equation fully so you can take steps to rectify the situation.

I covered this in depth in my book, *I Hope It Rains*, but I need to touch on this matter again to make sure that your nerves don't stem from this issue as it is a common cause of anxiousness related to riding. If you are in any way confused about competence playing a part in how you feel when riding, I have a very simple generalised example of how this competence/confidence equation works. If you are a very competent rider already, it may be a case that your nerves have stemmed from a different cause, not in any way linked to ability and are the type that you cannot easily identify or 'put your finger on'. For you, this chapter may not apply. It could be worth reading to further your understanding, but you will be able to address your fears using the workbooks rather than this section directly applying to you. I would urge you not to automatically assume you are a good rider, I know it is hard to self-evaluate but on this occasion, you need to be honest and look at the whole picture.

An extremely good rider should not feel nervous riding a very tricky / spooky /nappy / young / fresh / stubborn / hot/ un-schooled 'green' or newly backed horse. This is simply because they have the skills required to deal with everything the horse throws at them. Their skill is the key to their confidence. They may not be *happy* with a horse that bolts / bucks / naps etc, but they have the skills and knowledge to sort out the problem and educate the horse so he understands what is required of him in the future and the unacceptable behaviour is corrected with good training. Although these riders are more than likely not impressed by the behaviour and do not want it to go on uncorrected, they are not nervous and take it in their stride.

Let's not forget too that a good rider's ability is down to years of hard work, probably plenty of landings on their bum and their continued commitment to bettering themselves. A tenacious approach under the guidance of the best trainer they could afford or, in some rarer cases, just getting on and doing it, day after day (practise and commitment) working their way through the maze of horse training and riding. They have not found the magic wand of quick fix horsemanship (sadly, there isn't one) but just worked really, really hard using traditional, correct, time tested methods, not new-fangled, ego-fed rubbish put out by clever sales and advertising.

Just because someone has a 'name' or an enormous online following it does not necessarily make them knowledgeable or indeed any good in the real world. It worries me that some practitioners who aren't particularly fantastic or knowledgeable are easily masquerading as horse riding masters. They are cleverly manipulating social media and preying on an unquestioning audience who are often being given false hope and a false reality by these pseudo equestrian experts. Remember, a photograph is a millisecond of time and may have been set up with numerous takes until the desired shot was accomplished so do be aware. Yes, of course some are fabulous riders and trainers who should be applauded but always question the validity of what you are seeing and what you are buying into. It is sadly the case that many riders and trainers with real talent tend to be less visible to the masses. Perhaps they are not interested in portraying themselves as superstars and hunting desperately for 'followers' or 'likes' but are happy doing what they do, quietly training horses to a level of absolute excellence and working largely out of public view. These are the few who have real skill which has taken many years to perfect, unlike the constant 'party tricks' that we see being performed day in day out online.

Anyway, going back to the naughty/nappy/spooky or green horse. Let's imagine this same horse with a novice rider. It is almost certainly going to be a complete disaster. The novice rider does not yet have the skills of the experienced rider and the tricky horse is just simply beyond their capability at the moment. In fact, the horse is probably going to have them off fairly quickly if not potentially terrify them enough that they want to get off anyway. This is not because the horse is a demon, it is because he is a horse and he doesn't know until we teach him, what is right or wrong under saddle or in harness and what is acceptable when he is not at leisure in his field or stable.

A horse cannot lie, he will always do what he wants and thinks is right until we train and educate him in the most positive, kind, firm and fair way that we can. We must, as riders, know our limits. Over-horsing oneself is a huge problem, as is over-playing our hand as a rider. If you want to go and compete, do at least make sure you are setting yourself up for a positive experience by ensuring you are *capable* of riding to the degree expected before entering. Don't go in completely unprepared. A little out of your comfort zone is fine, it is good to push oneself but not to the point that it will be a horrible experience.

Take time to evaluate this matter. Be honest. Have you got a horse that is too much for your current stage of ability which, as much as you love him, is actually causing your fear of competing or going out in public? That might be the toughest question you have had to answer so far but most horse riders will have asked themselves this at some time. If the answer is 'yes' then don't despair, enlist the help of a friend or good instructor and work on the issues. You can get there, it may just be a longer route for you at present. Nothing worth having is easy, so hang in there and perhaps with practice, you could look to compete later in the year or further down the line, when you have had chance to rectify any issues and bring you and/or your horse up to scratch. Be warned that ego can play a part and that could be your downfall. Also, to be blunt, delusion can play a part. You may think you are better than you are. You must be honest with yourself in order to proceed and find success.

Those who have read my first book *I Hope It Rains* will have read how I bought a very naughty horse when I was far too novice to cope and despite my best efforts he had to be sold. It didn't feel like it at the time but it was the right thing to do for both our sakes. Having said that, give me that same horse now and I have no doubt I could cope with him and his antics fairly easily. He wouldn't have changed, but I have progressed as a rider and broken in and corrected plenty worse than him over the years. That ability is down to my hard work, hours in the saddle and confidence gained through competence. I have found time and time again, no matter how these horses are corrected, lots of them soon slip back to naughtiness once the less experienced rider gets back on board.

I do not condone selling every horse that challenges you or puts a foot wrong. I despise the culture of 'just get another one' with my entire soul, but there is a balance to be struck. Therefore, think this through and be honest with yourself. Is your horse too much for you? Ultimately only you can decide. There are options but you need to face up to facts first which is the most awful thing although in the long-run you will thank yourself for reaching the right conclusion.

If you conclude, like I once had to, heart-breakingly, that your horse is currently too much for you, then selling him on to a more suitable home may be what you think is best. However, here are some other ideas to consider:

Have someone else ride/compete him for you until you can improve or he can be taught what is needed for you to enjoy him fully at a later date. Be sensible though and go in to this with your eyes open. Having a professional or much better rider take the horse on for training will undoubtedly improve the horse and is a great idea in some instances. However, it will not necessarily make you capable of riding him unless you commit to learning too. In fact, the gap between his training and your ability could actually widen further.

I have seen this a thousand times, people think it is a quick route to glory or think that bad behaviour can be corrected sooner, which it can if the trainer is good. However, if you as a rider aren't up to the job of taking over the ride, many horses will revert – not because they are bad but because they can. People who have a professional ride their horse several times a week are often ultimately disappointed because the horse goes brilliantly, until they get on it. The situation unravels pretty quickly as the horse is more knowledgeable than the owner. It can be a complete disaster, emotionally because the owner no longer has a 'bond' with 'their' horse and physically in terms of the horse being able to do all sorts of wonderful things that the owner can't even begin to sit on. By training, I don't mean having lessons. Having a professional give you lessons will of course help you and the horse come to an understanding, it's the 'let someone else ride him and I will be OK too' scenario that isn't always going to work.

Turn him away for a while if he is young while you work on your problem areas and allow him to grow up and settle.

Loan him to a good, competent home so that you can have him back at a later date if you choose.

If funds allow, have a person loan him from the current yard so you still care for him and see him every day but get an additional horse that is more of a novice ride or more suited to your skill level at this current time. You can then work towards taking your horse back to ride in the future.

You must take notice of this equation, for if there is a deficit on your part in terms of skill, you are kidding yourself and holding yourself back. This is not the end of the world, just take some lessons or practise until you bring yourself up to scratch and can go to compete feeling completely in control and fully able to hold your own and have a fun, successful experience.

TYPES OF NERVES

Let's look firstly at the rider who competes regularly, doesn't get nervous as a rule but at a show or competition, feels 'suitably' nervous, anxious, perhaps has a bit of a dry mouth and is excited but is experiencing *similar* feelings to the ones you feel just thinking about going to a competition or filling out the entry form. So, the rider at the show naturally feels a little nervous but they still go in and do it anyway. Feeling apprehensive is normal. It is a reality for most sportsmen and women who want to do well. It is most likely borne out of excitement and passion for the sport or activity. Adrenaline in this form, when channelled correctly can give the person a competitive edge, that extra something for competition. We could refer to these as good nerves perhaps. The mind-set of this rider is possibly 'feel the fear and do it anyway' or more likely, they understand that the nerves will ease once they get down to business. They go in the arena or around the course and having performed well, it ends up being a fun, good experience and the positive mind-set cycle continues.

Over time the more shows, the more good results, the better they feel prepared both emotionally and physically, the better they will do. Also let's not forget the hours of practise they are putting in day to day with schooling and preparation. They are sensibly working hard, improving their skill-set as well as furthering the education and training of the horse so the whole picture becomes a good one, full of positivity and good results. It is very rarely down to luck. It is almost a given that it is down to dedication and hard work. As Jerry Barber, the famous golfer once said when asked why he was so lucky in competition: "the harder I practise the luckier I get". Says it all really doesn't it?

It is also important to realise everyone occasionally has a bad day and knocks a pole down or the horse trips in the personal show. They forget their dressage test or 'drift' in their thoughts going the wrong way on a course. However, because the rider is generally in a positive place, they can put the odd mishap down to a momentary lapse, an off-day, and move on without taking too much of an emotional battering. It may upset them at the time, we all make errors but the key to carrying on is knowing why it went wrong and trying to not let it happen again. The mind-set stays positive despite the 'blip', the competence/confidence equation stays balanced and everything ends well overall.

I am sure the reluctant competitor would be the first to point out that 'anyone would feel nervous at a show,' or riding a new horse on its debut, competing over a bigger jump course, moving up to a higher level, and they are right. The difference here is that you, the reluctant competitor beat yourself up for feeling this way. The rider with the 'normal' pre-performance jitters just gets on and does it, having dealt as best they can with the situation with training, planning and anything available to them to improve their chances, living for the euphoric, happy feeling after they have achieved their goal, however big or small it may be.

We must learn to realise that nerves are completely normal in unfamiliar or important circumstances. They are inevitable to a degree, when we are out of our comfort zone and not in a 'run of the mill' or definite situation. It is also worth remembering that some adrenalin and a *slight* nervousness can in fact give an edge to us for clear thinking and good performance. It is the crippling fear that is the enemy, not a few butterflies which are ultimately borne out of a desire to do well and completely expected at any level.

I'm not saying that anyone who feels fear thinking about entering or actually going to a competition isn't normal, let's get that straight. I am saying that we need to work with and understand the feelings so that the horrible, debilitating physical symptoms are considerably lessened with the techniques I will offer to you and become manageable and minimal so that you can carry on regardless. This will take time and practise but these nasty, unhelpful physical symptoms that have manifested from your anxiety can be overcome by recognising why we are fearful in order to start to rectify it. We need to make your competition riding more within your comfort zone so that provided you are competent and your horse is trained enough to do these things (again, I refer to the confidence/competence equation) your fears move in to the category of excited and full of anticipation rather than plain scared stiff.

SCORES AND RESULTS

It is very easy to get upset if the results, times or scores aren't quite what you had hoped for or imagined they would be. You have to remember, if you are putting yourself out there to be judged, you have to accept the viewpoint of that person as well as the physical factors that you cannot control. A horse will occasionally clip a pole or fence, a wrong approach will be made, a stride will be missed, he will drop out of canter at the wrong moment, etc. There are millions of scenarios and things beyond your control and you must not dwell on trying to manage everything because it is impossible. You must accept the unexpected and unplanned elements will crop up occasionally. That's life. It is not personal and sometimes you will do great, sometimes not so well and let's be honest, occasionally, you may have a complete disaster where it just goes plain wrong. We have all been there.

I had a young horse out at a ridden show and he was being a little difficult. To say he was over-excited would be an understatement and we just about managed to hold it together and get round. Our personal show was really good as he had actually settled by the time we got called out of the line-up but the 'go round' was, shall we say, quite an athletic display of all gaits, plus some squeals and bucks thrown in for good measure. At the prize giving (we got moved up from last to second place) the judge actually commented and said "well ridden, you were very calm and sympathetic to the horse which was nice to see. You helped the horse to settle and redeem himself, well done." I felt proud that I had done my best and acted well in a tough situation. I had not lost my temper with the horse, I was actually very accepting that this was a youngster and he had very little experience being out and about so my job was not to 'lose it' or get upset. I was the pilot and had to go with it, I had to do my best to calm him down and work with what we had. However, I think to the onlookers it was quite a spectacle.

Most riders, if they have competed regularly have had scores/results where they have been disappointed or elements of a test or show that haven't gone quite to plan and had to learn to accept the rollercoaster known as competing. It is often much easier to criticise others than look at where we are and why we are not hitting the mark. Nobody can win every time, nobody can be perfect every time. It is not realistic to expect perfection on every outing but as reluctant competitors, I think we can get drawn in to believing that 'other people' are doing everything perfectly all of the time. It is easy to blame the judge, blame the other competitors, blame the horse or blame ourselves but we must, despite our disappointment, have the sense to know that horses have their own minds and our job is to forge a strong enough partnership whereby they will be obedient and 'listen' to us in any situation (eventually).

Similarly, I took my four-year-old stallion to a very low-key show jumping competition as I thought it was a good opportunity for him to see some jumps and little fillers and work in an indoor arena for the first time. It was great experience to go out, all dressed up and do a couple of clear rounds followed by a 'baby' competition. We actually went clear until I caught a half-sized plastic jump wing with my foot but, despite me demolishing the jump, it was a good day and well worth the effort. The next time we went back to the indoor school for some working equitation, he was far more settled as he had been there before. Although I think he was surprised the jumps from the previous event had turned in to all kinds of obstacles, he was a good boy and took it in his young stride.

Try not to put off having a go. I know it is nerve wracking and will take a lot of courage but it is worth it and one day when it is 'second nature' you will be so glad you went that first time. Of course it takes time and training so before we get to that place of 'perceived perfection' there will be ups and downs, but it is the same for everyone. One thing we must have is a sense of humour and, especially important, good grace in success or defeat. I know it's tough but try to learn from your mistakes and if being judged, accept that the opinion of one person, on one day is just that. It is hard not to take things to heart, but don't. It isn't worth it in the long run. Just chalk it up to experience and fight another day. However it turned out, it was an experience, one that will never be repeated, that day has gone and will never come back. Treat it as part of the richness of life and move on.

FEAR OF LOSING

This is a side to nerves that is difficult to come to terms with but certainly, for many competitive people, a real issue that can cause problems later down the line if it isn't dealt with. The problem of being afraid to lose may sound strange. Of course we will win and lose, that is the nature of sport, right? Yes, it is, but for those who suffer from this, it is usually because of their pride being hurt rather than because they are megalomaniacs or power-crazed competitors. Not wanting to lose is natural, it is why we compete – in order to win. However, for some, losing is a really difficult thing to get over and may actually stop them from competing in the future if they cannot recover from the loss. It is a great tragedy if your horse is primed and you have the skills to do really well but your mind-set lets your pride be so damaged with defeat that you don't want to take part in your sport anymore. I think for people who suffer with this side of anxiety, it is the fear of people labelling them a 'loser' or saying things like "he obviously isn't as good as he thought".

We are taught that having damaged pride is bad, embarrassing and unacceptable, but actually is it? If you have taken great care in your training and all the preparation leading up to competition, of course you will have dented pride if it doesn't go so well. If we are honest, who wouldn't feel this way? The problem occurs when a person's pride is so damaged they can't see a way back from it, they can't deal with it. I think this is different from ego as ego can be a 'big headed', self-important trait whereas, I see pride as a gentler part of our being. Pride is the part of us that cares about what we are doing and means we go the extra mile, double checking everything, polishing our boots before a competition and making sure we are as good as we can be in order to give it our best shot.

As competitors, we do go out there to do well and, once we are performing, giving it our all, we definitely want to be number one. However, we can't all be winners all the time. There will always be elements or people who we come up against who just do beat us for whatever reason. It is hard to swallow at the time but the key is to make the losses count for the future wins. If you lose or don't place as highly as you expected, it doesn't necessarily mean that the other person is better than you, it just means that you'll have to approach the next competition differently or train that particular element harder to overcome it. Win or lose, or as it should be referred to: 'win or learn.' Prepare yourself to cope with losing by accepting it as part of sport. Don't let it get you down or destroy you for the future. It is one time out of many, there is no need to be absolutely devastated and never be able to continue. Losing is part of life and it is an opportunity to see what the problem is and grow from it.

This amusing quote could pretty much apply to any area of competing:

"Dressage, the only sport where you completely lose the ability to ride or remember anything and pay someone to point out all your mistakes in public."

Unknown

Your peers shouldn't judge you harshly or be unkind about a result that you were disappointed about. Genuine friends will wish you better luck next time. Nine times out of ten, while you are dwelling on a score or result, the people around you won't be and probably won't even remember what it was a week down the line, let alone judge you because of it. One thing that is important is always to remain sportsman-like. There is nothing more undignified than a bad loser.

I was at a show where a competitor who clearly expected to win and was full of her own importance demonstrated this rather aptly. As it turned out, this person came second from last in quite a large class of what she clearly originally considered was full of lowly or less able competitors. She was nothing short of unprofessional from start to finish and it was not pleasant to witness. From trying to cut everyone up and intimidate them, loudly tutting and huffing, then complaining about the judge while still in the ring, it was awful and should never have happened. By all means think what you like but don't say it. She then, to make matters worse, stormed out of the ring before the steward invited the line-up to do so, which was not only disrespectful to the other competitors and the judge, but unnecessary. Then, after storming off the show ground, that evening she posted on social media complaining about the show, moaning about the other competitors and the judge. Everyone is entitled to an opinion but to air it is usually unnecessary and in this instance very undignified.

Most shows will have a complaints procedure which you can follow if there is a genuine grievance but this is generally a case of doing so in writing and, to be clear, a genuine grievance is not coming further down the line up than you hoped you would. This competitor inadvertently drew attention to her 'defeat' and her bad behaviour and appalling attitude stuck in the minds of many a long time after the actual placing would have been forgotten. Case in point that I am mentioning it here and it was a few years ago. Personally I don't agree she should have come so far down the line up. For what it's worth, she had a lovely horse, well-turned out and he was well-mannered. However, the judge obviously preferred the rest of us. We shall never know why, but whatever the reason, don't behave like her.

Have grace, dignity and good manners whilst endeavouring to be a good loser. We will all have disappointing days from time to time but hopefully they are few and far between. A good way to deal with scores or results is to set your own benchmarks. If you are doing a ridden show, why not try to perfect your personal show so that each time you compete it is more polished. You may not always get a judge that favours your horse but if you know you have done the best you can, the horse was well-turned out, well-behaved and well-ridden it is actually a great achievement irrespective of your position in the line-up. Reflect on the positives and when you go to your next show or event, try to build up the presentation and take on board any pointers or comments from the previous judge to show off this time.

It is the same with dressage. Make a note of your own scores and strive to beat your personal best next time. It is the same with jumping. Only compete against yourself and make a note of your results/times in a journal to look back on. Keep count of clear rounds and look at the list with pride. Competing against yourself is the only way of ensuring a level playing field: you against yourself. You may have come first or last but if your scores and results are on the whole improving, your technique and overall appearance looking better, then it's all good and going in the right direction.

Try not to fall into the trap of comparing yourself with others all the time. It is ok to be competitive and make comparisons up to a point, but not so you make yourself unhappy or feel your self-worth has been negatively impacted. It is important to remember, whether you are a super competitive person or someone who literally wants to go out as and when they fancy it, riding is supposed to be fun, it is your hobby and you should not be doing things that make you unhappy.

Life is hard enough without heaping so much pressure on yourself that competing, or more likely the result, becomes the be all and end all.
Try to keep it in perspective, respond and learn from the negatives and build yourself up from the positives. Most of all keep smiling and enjoying what you are doing. Always compete for you and never get angry or cross, nor take it out on your horse. Ever.

DO YOUR HOMEWORK

It is more sensible to start low key than get upset about the challenge and end up not doing any shows at all. Do some dressage, showing, jumping, eventing or whatever you fancy at a private yard competition, at home with some like-minded horsey friends and a willing 'judge', or go out of your immediate area to compete at a lower level than that to which you aspire. Don't over-face yourself, downgrade a level and just have one aim for the day - **go, take it as it comes and enjoy it**. Feel the uplifting joy of your progression as you learn your craft, hone your skills and work on your competing prowess. The fantastic, happy feeling you will have once your horse learns his job and is responsive to your aids, soft in your hand, willing in his steps and confident in his ability is beyond compare and it will be worth the wait.

In the early days, if you really are wracked with nerves, just going, tacking up and getting on at a show is a step in the right direction. Do not let any achievement, however minor it may appear, detract from the fact that you are moving forward in a positive way. Have you thought about taking your horse to the show just to ride in the collecting ring (provided this is practical and allowed)? You will feel involved in the day but without the pressure. Maybe after you have done this you will think, "Well, I got that far so I may as well compete next time." These small positive experiences will inspire you to have another go tomorrow, the next day, the next week and so on. Through positive experience, the fear and anxiety will naturally subside because your mind is no longer in a situation where it is associating the task with all those stored up negative emotions which the brain finds hard to process and dispose of. You may have the odd set back but stick to your guns and push on. You will be amazed how quickly it all starts to come together.

It is important when you do venture to your first competitive venue that you feel you have accomplished something at the end of the day. At no point beat yourself up emotionally whatever the outcome. Always try to finish on a positive note so that your horse goes back to his stable happy and you feel that you have had some fun and achieved something good. "Rome was not built in a day."

Whether you are showing, eventing, show jumping, doing dressage, TREC, or anything else for that matter, do your homework. I don't mean in terms of practising the riding elements. I assume that if you are going to compete that you are doing that anyway at home. By 'do your homework,' I mean scope out the venue, suss out what other competitors at your level do and watch the classes. It is really useful to watch classes at your own level to give a good idea of what happens, what judges expect and the level of training that the horse and rider should have reached in order to participate successfully. A note of caution if you do watch, and you aren't quite ready, don't let it stop you trying if you can accept that you are there to take part, just for the experience and you may or may not place highly (amazing job if you do).

At the more advanced levels or larger shows, watch the seasoned competitors too. It is a great way to look at how they deal with things and a nice day out with no pressure. Watch closely, pay attention to their ring craft. At senior levels this should be polished and the insight they can give the amateur or novice competitor is very valuable. Be careful not to over-inflate what is expected at your level though. Watch and learn what goes on in the advanced classes, but do keep grounded and realistic. These riders have more than likely had many years of practise and experience and would probably be the first to admit that when they first started out, they were not as polished and accurate as they are now. Practise, determination and steady progression is the key to success but remember that everyone had to start somewhere and everyone, from the local show to the seasoned pro had to have a 'first time'. By watching the level you want to compete at and the more advanced riders, it should give you a balanced reality check about what is expected, what happens and how to deal with the event you are wishing to participate in.

Many years ago, I was definitely guilty of thinking I wasn't able to compete because I spent time watching top level performance and rightly thought, "I can't do that." Well of course I couldn't, I was watching the 2000 Sydney Olympic Games! What I needed to remember, and nobody pointed out, was to watch the seniors for inspiration and watch your own peer group for realistic 'where I'm at' benchmarks so that you can set your bar as well as have a goal for the future. I was too terrified to even try to enter a class on my little cob because I let everything snowball in my head. I thought I had to be perfect to compete and kept putting it off and off until, through old age and lameness he retired and I had lost the chance forever. I was lucky, I had many more chances to have another go with other horses, initially riding for work on grand prix dressage, jumping and equivalent working equitation horses which gave me the skills needed to ride youngsters and bring my own horse on with strict and constant guidance from a top flight rider and trainer.

I realised that despite having access to incredibly talented and schooled older horses, starting at the bottom and working my way up was the only way for me, although I realise that for some that is not the case and to buy an already-trained horse is not a crime. It is great to have a dream but actually, don't let the dream become bigger than the reality and scare you so much that you don't take that first step to have a go in the ring or on the course. I will also say in defence of people who are lucky enough to have a school master, it is up to them at what level they choose to compete provided within the rules of the individual competition or governing body. It may seem odd that a former advanced horse is now doing a much lower level with their current owner, but live and let live. You are probably not in possession of all the facts and it may well be that the horse has an old injury or is now at an age where for welfare reasons it is no longer ethical or appropriate to push him hard. It may also be that the current rider does not have the experience and has indeed purchased the horse to help them grow as a competitor and allow them to fulfil their dreams. Each to their own. It is very important to remember that comparing you to yourself is the best way. Just aim to improve your scores and results as you will not be up against the same horses and riders indefinitely. Enjoy the moment, wherever you come in the final placing and whatever you are riding. Your horse is your best friend so don't put him down, always love him and be proud of him.

Another top tip is go and see where you will be competing. Scoping out a venue or watching others is just plain sensible but it is amazing how many people don't use a 'recce' to their advantage and just turn up on the day with their nerves even more on edge because they don't know what to expect or where to go. It is stressful enough getting ready for a show or event, travelling a horse and driving to the venue without adding to the worry by not knowing where you are going. Take any chance you can to diminish nerves. From looking at the route map in advance to leaving in plenty of time to travel. If possible, maybe do a 'dry run' before-hand as anything you do will always be a bonus. Knowing the route to drive somewhere is a must, especially when taking a lorry or trailer. Knowing the lay out of the facilities may seem almost trivial but can give you such peace of mind on the day. It will make you feel so much better just knowing where the secretary's office is, where to park or where the loo is rather than worrying at the last minute.

Some good advance planning will give you immeasurable peace of mind. Turning up on the spur of the moment is fine if you are a spontaneous or 'feel the fear and do it anyway' kind of person, but for most, a simple trip out to have a look round and see the 'lie of the land' will improve confidence and encourage you to go another day actually to participate, feeling you are armed with some knowledge of the destination. Even if you can't physically go to the venue, go online and suss it out on Google Earth, at least you can see the layout to a degree. Watching a class and standing there thinking "I could do that," is where you want to be emotionally, so visiting and watching is a great way of stacking the odds in your favour in terms of planning and reducing 'on the day' nerves for the future.

One last, probably obvious piece of advice is take a friend with you if you find it too daunting a task going alone. Some people do prefer to just go it alone. I totally get that, I have often gone off to competitions on my own but this tended to be later on when I knew more what was expected and knew the venues. I think mostly, when going anywhere new, it is usually a good idea to have another pair of hands, just someone you can call on to go and grab a cup of tea or sign you in before your class. It is the little things that can be tricky. You have a horse that needs tacking up but also need a pair of eyes watching the classes before you so you know when to make your way over to the collecting ring, or keeping a note of times so you know when you are 'on.' A friend can be worth their weight in gold.

Dare I say it? Be a bit picky. Don't take the friend who is more nervous than you are as they will do nothing to calm you down. Even if they are salt of the earth and well meaning, their nerves will definitely rub off on you and that will no doubt mean you are stressing before you even arrive, let alone get in the ring or on the course. Try to take someone who will calm you down, know how to help without being over the top and genuinely wants to be with you and watch you do well. A non-horsey friend may work well for some. You know your friends so you can decide, but be mindful that tempers can snap a little and silly arguments can blow up in stressful situations when someone well-meaning is asking a million questions and getting in the way in the name of trying to be helpful. Nothing is worth falling out over so do try to be restrained and calm if you can.

With a little forward planning, plenty of pre-event practise and some talking yourself in to it, you will no doubt have a good day and who knows, you might do better than you had ever hoped.

PLAY TO YOUR STRENGTHS

There are a lucky few who have a horse that can turn its hoof to anything. You know the ones, today they are off eventing, tomorrow showing and next week doing Western, pleasure rides or TREC. This may seem like the impossible dream, but, at entry to medium level disciplines, a nicely put together, fit, mannerly and well-trained horse by definition should be able to do most if not all things required. Of course, generally as you progress, it will become obvious that a horse may have more talent for one thing than another but we often see race horses that have performed well on the track having a great second career eventing, doing dressage, endurance etc. Yes, there will be things some horses are better at than others. A horse that is seen to excel in jumping will no doubt follow that path but, for the average person, having a go at a few things is a really good way of seeing what suits you both best. You don't have to put yourselves in a self-limiting 'box'. Don't be afraid to mix it all up from time to time. You never know, you may find a new sport that you absolutely love and, within reason, your horse will enjoy the change of scene.

Having a go is the only way to find out what suits you. For example, in the course of a summer, why not go to a local show, do some in-hand or ridden classes, enter a dressage test at a suitable level for your training, go and do some eventing at the local riding club or head to the forest or beach for some pleasure rides. Do whatever takes your fancy. Pick the things you liked best to try again. You may find that, like lots of people, enjoying lots of different disciplines is what you enjoy best. There is nothing wrong with this at all if it works for you and your horse. I knew a lady who was actually very novice in terms of riding but was keen as keen could be and had a very nice mare who would literally turn her hoof to anything. The mare was kind and forgiving and every weekend they were off trying something new. They didn't shine at any one thing, but were so happy enjoying all that horse sport has to offer. Despite never moving up any levels (I don't believe she wanted to), they were content and enjoyed life to the max trying as many new things as possible, from horse-ball, cross country, agility, working equitation, TREC and dressage to penning cattle at a western event.

In the end, most people find something they enjoy more, or something their horse is better at and tend to go with it, but don't feel pressured to pick one thing and stick to it if that is not what you want to do. There may be an element of 'jack of all trades, master of none' but does it matter if you are having fun and the horse is enjoying himself too? To progress with something you love will be a joy, while if you don't enjoy it or have a flair for it, it will probably not be as much fun and you are unlikely to stick at it. Fun is a key word. We spend all our money, our spare time and our lives caring for and looking after our horses, so whatever discipline you enjoy, from ground work, liberty or ridden, it should be fun. If it isn't you really should look at why it is not enjoyable and perhaps re-evaluate what has gone wrong. As equestrians, united by our love of horses, we must always keep fun in the forefront of our minds.

When you have found the area that suits you best, you can further hone your skills by training hard, watching and learning as much as possible. For example, I have suggested watching classes at your own and higher levels. Evaluate the riders and by *evaluate* I do not mean be bitchy and uber-critical. Don't be an armchair expert who spouts criticism. It is not nice nor necessary. However, you can mentally critique another rider to help you progress with your own performance. There is a fine line between being cocky or inappropriate and evaluating another person's performance to help understand the sport and enhance your own riding. I always say ride for yourself and only look at your own results and I stand by that but sometimes, if you are a watching another rider, maybe you can judge them as if in a kind of pseudo competition, watch them ride and see what mistakes they make. More importantly, see how they correct these issues and learn from this for your own future performance. You don't have to be nasty to do an evaluation. We pay to enter a class and ask a judge to do it all the time so why not do it yourself? Only you can ensure it doesn't become a session of putting someone else down for your own ends. This is why I suggest you evaluate them privately, in your own thoughts. Don't air your findings, just use them to your advantage so that they remind you to sit up straight, use the corners, not flap your legs, shorten the stride or anything that will help you in competition. Keep these thoughts private and safely filed away in your sub-conscious repertoire. Under no circumstances, even if somebody you are watching is having the worst day, make fun or be nasty. It could be any of us so remember: pride comes before a fall...

There are a million little things you can do to improve your ring craft. Think strategically to give you some edge and allow as much chance of success as possible. Play to your strengths within your current level of training. For example, if you are doing a dressage to music plan and your horse excels in a medium trot, ensure that this is right in front of the judge and use it to gain marks. If your right canter transition is not as good as the left, put the movement away from the judge and minimise it as much as you can. This is not cheating, trust me, you won't hide anything from a good judge, but it is picking the things you want to show off and putting the things you need to work on to one side as it were. If it is a pre-determined test, I'm afraid you are stuck with it, but in the early days, use the tricky floorplans at home to train and pick a test you are confident with for your trips out. As they say, "train hard, compete easy."

The same goes for a floor plan when showing. If your horse can do a lovely simple or flying change, be sure to do it right in front of the judge. If not, think about how to show off the transitions in a neat and controlled way. Maybe come back to trot earlier if you need more time to ride the transition or if you need less time but still need the assistance of the 'loop.' Keep the canter longer so it is not right under the nose of the judge and then once over the centre, transition to trot so that once in the 'corner' or on the loop of the figure of eight you can ask for canter. With the correct aids and correct bend, you will be able to pick up the correct canter lead more easily. Whatever you do, try not to 'drop' the horse in the downward transitions or 'grab' his mouth in the upward ones.

Where you are able to do your own plan there is scope to make it work for you in a very precise way. Even if it is different from other competitors, try it out. If the judge doesn't like it, briefly ask how you can improve and what they would like to see. They can't hold a long, or in-depth conversation in the ring but will definitely be able to give you a quick pointer while doing the prize giving. It is worth remembering that anything involving a show is subjective and it is the opinion of that judge on that day. It may not be the opinion of all others in the future so don't take criticism to heart. Work with it, learn from it and move on.

For show jumping, eventing, working equitation, trail, TREC or anything with pre-set courses, obviously you are not at liberty to move things around to suit, but you can still plan and can still do your homework by mixing up the training at home and understanding what strengths you have as a rider and what strengths your horse has. If you need more space to turn in to certain jumps or obstacles, try to see the best way of achieving that when you walk the course. Walking the course isn't for chatting, it is to plan your attack on each fence/obstacle, to find the line that suits you, to count the strides required, to work out where to lengthen and shorten and turn so that you have a good chance of getting everything right. The good thing with jumps and obstacles, it is not as subjective, it is more based on actual fact. If you topple a pole or knock something, you pay in faults or penalties, if you go clear you are clear and there is nothing anyone can say except "well done."

As a note of caution, try not to let time get to you. Speed rounds or 'against the clock' should mean go as quickly as you can within the realms of capability, not hare round and mess it up completely because you get fixated with speed and overcook it. I have done it myself in a speed round where, all of a sudden, getting too focussed on the speed meant I dropped points by not remembering to ride the course properly or accurately. The old saying, 'more haste, less speed' is very true so don't give up vital points for extra seconds if it means you will pay in mistakes.

Until the horse is properly trained, flying around at 'mach-3' can be very detrimental as you could inadvertently de-train him and 'heat him up' by riding poorly and thus 'teaching' him incorrectly. It is better to try and take a little more time and be careful as you often find that the score at the end, within reason, will reflect the accuracy just as much, if not more than the time score. If you were fast but messy it will be a worse score than a not quite so quick but 'clean' and accurate round. As you improve you can increase speed and then you are going to see very fast times with accurate results. Never sacrifice accuracy for speed while a horse is young or learning or you are learning. You will not thank yourself in the long term.

SPE (SELF PROCLAIMED EXPERT)

For those of you who have read my first book *I Hope It Rains, The Confidence Manual for the nervous rider*, you will probably remember the chapter on SPEs. Well, here we are again. SPEs crop up not only at the yard or in your 'horsey social circle', they are at shows too! Hooray! I hear you cry. One thing is certain, these people never miss the chance of offering their wisdom and loud, over-zealous 'encouragement' in public as well as in private. Oh joy! For those who are new to the 'phenomenon' that is the SPE, I will explain all.

SPEs are self-proclaimed experts. The people who know everything about everything but still manage mostly never to sit on a horse for any length of time or do anything very constructive when they do. Often, despite talking a good game, if they do ride, it's often not very effectively. These are the people to be avoided, although trying to avoid them is like outrunning a heat-seeking missile. They would advise a top rider from the safety of the ground and no doubt will take any chance they can find to advise you and everyone else in the arena or ring too. You know who they are. When they are at the yard or invite themselves over to your place to watch you ride, they are the ones who are constantly leaning on the arena fence being annoying, swigging fizzy pop, eating crisps or snacks but at the same time advising you loudly and without invitation. A lack of skill doesn't stop them either, they talk as if they have just been round Burghley Horse Trials last weekend and are off to set the world alight again this weekend. They talk as if they are grand prix riders and can offer wisdom straight from the pages of the latest book or magazine they have read, if you are lucky. If not, wisdom from deep within their 'elite equestrian minds.' They love a new fad or fashion and never understand why you are taking things slowly and steadily.

Mostly they are harmless, well-intentioned individuals, but let's face it, they can't actually do any of what they are talking about and the ones who can have a saint of a horse that gives them the flying change or correct canter lead because he can. The horse knows the quickest route back to the stable or field is to be compliant under saddle, help them show off and get back to eating, but I digress. Now, stop smirking because the person at the yard you are thinking about may also be at the show or event and, understandably, this is not ideal and could put you off. Let's hope not, but inevitably they will at some point turn up, probably without a horse as the horse just gets in the way of handing out sage advice to the masses. At the edge of the ring they can impart tips by loudly saying really helpful things like "it's on the wrong leg" (just in case the judge missed it), "that transition wasn't very smooth," "that show was too long/short," "she didn't go up the centre line very straight" and "she missed the stride at that fence" amongst many other criticisms. Wasn't that helpful?

What we have to do is ignore them. I know it's almost impossible but if you let your ear tune in to them and their sniping comments just as you go in the ring or enter the arena, you have every chance of being distracted, flustered and suddenly feel you are under pressure and that is not helpful. Remember one thing, you are in there having a go and they are not. End of. Do not listen to them, do not take their comments on board (the judge is there to do the judging, not them) and most of all do not take the bait by answering them back or worst still, arguing. It will serve no purpose except to put your heart rate through the roof, which will go straight down the reins to the horse, spoil your day and squash any chance of a relaxed, prize-winning ride.

Whether you are competing locally or internationally, one thing is for sure. Armchair SPEs are out there. At any level and in any sport. At best it is an opinion to which they are entitled. At worst it's absolute rubbish (or insert rude word of your choice). You will hear or read their thoughts in real time as you go round or no doubt later too, on social media. Ignore everything. As your Nan probably said, "if you can't say anything nice, don't say anything at all." This is that moment. Block them out and enjoy yourself, and if you are "on the wrong leg" then as long as you know, you can work at fixing it for next time.

Don't let these people spoil your day and your chances. They will pick on anyone and usually end up discussing the whole line up, from not liking the colour of a competitor's jacket to not liking the colour of a horse or the type of saddle. You name it, they will know best. Part of me wants to say that maybe they have their own nerves and that is why they don't compete and that is why they are so forthright and opinionated about everyone else to mask their own short-comings. I know that we are taught to be non-judgemental and all-inclusive but when it comes to these people, from experience there is generally no hope that being nice will work. So, like all bullies, there is nothing for them to feed off if you ignore them. That's the hard bit, so good luck, but it is worth it.

However, having picked on the SPE, do not under-estimate the power of groups in a positive way, provided they are made up of kind people who genuinely want to have fun and grow their skill set together by supporting each other as well as competing against one another. Don't lose sight of the fun element. Laughing and being part of a group can strengthen you. Many yards run 'have a go' days or private 'yard only' shows for show jumping, dressage, jump cross, cross country, working equitation, western trail, cattle and all sorts. Maybe enter one of these shows at your yard and encourage each other. It really can help not trying to cope alone and having a laugh with (not at) each other is good medicine and a positive experience, so don't rule it out. Laughter and support for one another is a great tonic and you will also realise that everyone has their demons and struggles with certain aspects of riding or have things they don't like doing as much. Once you realise you are not alone in having some reservations, you will start to progress more quickly and see everything from a much brighter perspective.

HONESTY

Before we get in to the exercises, let's think about two things. Firstly, nervous does not necessarily mean novice. It is a misconception that beginners, the novices, are the worried ones. This simply is not true. An experienced, excellent rider who outwardly exhibits great skill on a horse can be just as nervous, in terms of competing, as a complete novice or somebody who isn't as capable as they would like to be at present. Secondly, we must look at excuses and reasons. I refer to procrastination, in whatever form it manifests (not being ready to compete because you don't feel good enough, you want to train a little more before entering, you cannot get the correct canter lead, you are concerned about the shape of your circles, you may forget the course, test etc) as a **reason** for not competing rather than an **excuse**. For reluctant competitors, it is mostly a case of desperately wanting to enter but anxiety, worry, nerves, call them what you will, stop them in their tracks. An excuse is, by my reckoning, something we don't want to do or can't be bothered to attempt, very different from someone who is crippled with nerves and "what ifs" not being able to go through with entering a class.

We have looked at why a rider would be nervous or have butterflies at a show and addressed how to deal with it, but if your issues are more serious, let's do the first exercise and get on the road to sorting this out once and for all. I re-iterate, there are no quick fixes, it is down to honesty and hard work on your part but you can change your outlook and re-wire your mind-set. There's no point trying to do this while you are juggling the laptop and phone, chatting with friends, walking the dog, cooking dinner, or in any situation where you are unable to focus 100% on the matter in hand. You need to complete this task in four parts and each requires concentration, honesty and patience. So, if you can find a quiet hour or so, you can begin with step 1. I know, finding that free time may be a challenge in itself but hang in there!

Getting over and establishing the cause of fears

Until you can say this sentence, or something similar out loud to yourself, you cannot easily progress. Say it, feel it, acknowledge it, but don't judge yourself "I want to get over my fear of competing and I must establish the cause."

It's not easy to be honest with ourselves sometimes. If you felt awkward even saying that sentence and 'facing up' to it don't be disheartened as it is a step in the right direction. If you cried, felt deflated, silly or didn't feel anything at all, that's ok too. Just go with it for now. This is a little piece in the jigsaw, no pressure, just honesty and acceptance. It may sound a little 'out there' or new age, but loving and accepting ourselves for who we are is a very important step to dealing with anything that is upsetting us or holding us back.

Find a suitable place for soul searching. It may be the garden, indoors at the dining room table or in a comfy chair. Wherever it is, it must be with no distractions. You really need to take this seriously, and not when you are in a hurry, angry or flustered. Take a good old fashioned note pad or four sheets of paper and prepare four columns (or one on each page). This is going to be your workbook in which you explore, analyse and discover the root causes of your anxieties and come up with realistic, workable solutions. It will be a highly personal piece of self-analysis and unfortunately, until you can be honest with yourself, you will be unable to progress properly, so don't be afraid to pour your heart out on to the page. It is crucial to be really honest but also very important that you don't get cross with yourself for admitting what upsets you. Don't leave something off the list or not write it down because if someone else reads it you would feel embarrassed or that you were making a fuss over nothing. Nobody else ever needs to see your workbook unless you choose to share it so be open and write it all down.

Every last thing that worries you about the thought of competing, from filling the form in to actually going to the venue and doing the show/test/course should go on to this list. If you have an outpouring of emotion, it doesn't matter, nobody will know anyway, but even if they did, they will not judge you as harshly as you will no doubt judge yourself. Sometimes tears are part of the healing process, they show that you are passionate, that you care and that you want to mend the situation you are currently in. For anyone that got this far and then cried, this is me sending you a big 'virtual' hug and saying "ok, don't worry, you can do this". Relax, go with it and start writing the first column.

You may be amazed that once you are committed to writing things down and dealing with the issues, how easy it flows from your heart to the page and for some there will be almost an instant clarification of the underlying problem. For others it will come but take a little more time and attention. You can add to your workbook any time as feelings unravel, but get started with what comes to mind initially. Sit back and let the uncertainties and worries come to the surface. As busy people we are all so used to brushing things aside and having a stiff upper lip and carrying on. In this case, do the opposite, which is why it is important to give yourself enough time alone for this part of the exercise. If something 'strange' or unexpected crops up, don't not write it down because it seems odd, just go with it. This is about complete openness and honesty and you may be amazed that what manifests as one feeling, actually stems from something completely different from that which you thought.

Column 1 – What scares me?

I have just given examples but your Column 1 will be specific to your riding discipline, it may include things like those shown on list below but there is no right or wrong, just note down anything that feels right for you and reflects your feelings.

I cannot say how long your list will be. What I can say is that when you write it all down you must not be worried if it is a couple of things or a whole long list. Being honest with yourself at this stage is the key to future success. There are thousands of reasons, far too many to list here but try and describe your problem accurately. If there are several problems, you may possibly see a link where they are stemming from one underlying issue. If it is one issue or more, you can group them together in the next few columns and any fears that stem from the same reason can be dealt with as one. Any fear that is not related to the other feelings will be dealt with separately, by using another workbook (following the same format) to work through that issue on its own. Stick with me, I will explain this as we go through.

For illustrative purposes I have picked the topic which I can relate to from my past experience. Also from my research, it seemed to be a common worry. Obviously your list will be completely personal to you and you can tailor your workbook to match your issue which is how it can work for anyone in any discipline.

I am scared I won't know what to do in the show
I am worried I will go the wrong way in the cross country
I am scared I will look silly if I get something wrong
I am scared to canter in the ridden show
I am afraid of being judged
I am afraid to ride in front of a crowd

- I don't think I am as skilled as other competitors
- I don't want to have to face negative remarks or judgements
- I am worried the judge will think I am not good enough to be there
- I am scared I will forget my test/course/route/personal show
- I am afraid that people watching will mock me or laugh
- I am scared that once I am in the arena I will go blank and forget what I am meant to do
- I haven't done it before and I am worried I will do something incorrectly
- I don't cope well with the added pressure of being in the spotlight
- I don't even really think I want to but feel pressured to compete

Column 1 'WHAT' WHAT IT IS THAT SCARES ME	Column 2	Column 3	Column 4
I want to do a dressage test but am too scared to try			

I know it's hard to face up to a fear, let alone write it down, so if you have done that you should be very happy with yourself that you have taken this first step and are heading in the right direction. For once, give yourself some credit and proudly acknowledge that you have been really brave, you have written down your fears and, possibly for the first time, actually faced them. You have taken a positive step to beating your anxiety and that is brilliant and I applaud you.

Column 2 – Why does it scare me?

Take a moment to read the list in column 1, but don't dwell on it. Let's look at what causes the initial feelings of fear. In the second column write down the detail behind the fear: the 'why'. The reason that the anxiety has started, snowballed out of control and now strikes you with absolute horror when you think about it, let alone try to do the thing that scares you.

For example, if you wrote 'I want to do a dressage test but am too scared to try,' the detail behind this would be looking at why you are afraid of that scenario, exploring the feelings connected to the fear. Don't just list the obvious things. The answer often lies in the real deep-down feelings. You need to take time on these exercises, dig deep and really think about each problem in turn. If there are several issues, you will have to work through each one separately, but that's fine, it can be done over a period of time. However, where possible, try to do as much of your list as you can in one sitting. Be honest, be open and do not feel any shame about your answers and findings.

To give some examples. I have used one scenario of competing in an arena or ring but of course any problem in any discipline can be dealt with in this way.

Whatever it is that you have identified, by putting the 'why' in the second column you are starting to break the problem down and understand it better. Do try not to over think things though, what matters at this early stage is that you are being honest with yourself, facing your emotions and fears and trying to do something constructive about getting past the issue. Turning negative thoughts into a positive mind-set will in time become your general outlook and help find the harmony you so dearly want and of course, DESERVE. The legendary, international show-jumper, the late Mr Tim Stockdale once gave some advice to a good friend of mine. He was questioning whether he should keep and compete an incredibly talented jumping horse he had purchased as an amateur rider. The words stuck with me years later when I also had a wobble about owning an incredibly well-bred, talented youngster that I thought was too good for me to own let alone compete. He said "everyone deserves one top horse in their lifetime. It doesn't matter how good you are or what level you are at. If the horse is yours, you deserve to have it and enjoy it, stop worrying what other people think and get on with riding it."

I think this is a great sentiment, it certainly changed my attitude from one of great caution "I don't want to mess the horse up" to "Do you know what? I own this horse, I love him, I paid for him, I backed him and I school him to the best of my ability. So yes, damn right I deserve to have him and I will do well on him." Guess what? As soon as I got my head round that, we started to do very well and continue to do so. The imaginary shackles had been removed and I started to believe in myself and realise that I was good enough. What's more, you're good enough too, you just need to escape the self-doubt prison that you own mind has very un-helpfully put you in!

Column 1 'WHAT' WHAT IT IS THAT SCARES ME?	Column 2 'WHY' WHY DOES IT SCARE ME?	Column 3	Column 4
I want to do a dressage test but am too scared to try	I will look silly if it goes wrong or I mess something up I should be doing better than I am I have been riding years! I dare not even try, the thought turns me to jelly! I don't believe I can do it My horse is green so he might play up half way through the test I feel inadequate I am not as good or experienced as other competitors I am afraid to try in case I forget the next move I can never get the correct diagonal (!) My horse is not as athletic or advanced as the others so I may not look good enough What if I have a melt-down and want to leave the		

	arena half way through People will make fun of me as I have no experience		

Column 3 - Thinking about the fear and the emotions behind it

Go through your list in its entirety, take on board what you have written and now do a third column to start to investigate the fear and how it has become an issue for you. Are there factors that link your fears? Is there more than one thing that worries you? As I said earlier, we have to look for links to see if there is a competence issue or a factor that runs clearly through your problems which, although it manifests in different ways, actually stems from one or two things. The third column is the one we use to put the fears into perspective and try to rationalise them. Break them down and see if we can diminish them by looking at them more clearly.

If your fear is borne of an accident, you will need to really dig deep to work through this issue, but the fact that you have got this far means you must want to succeed. This is a positive and you should be proud of yourself for trying to sort things out. Just go steady and take one step at a time to build a solid foundation from which to work.

The list is just an example, your own list will be more personal and in depth, but you get the general idea of writing down the initial fear/problem and breaking it down step by step. There is no right or wrong with your lists, just be honest and open minded and go with it. In column 3 you need to look at the problem in some ways as if you are another person looking at your problem from a clearer perspective. Imagine what you would tell someone if your fear was theirs and they had come to you for advice. This may sound odd but you would be surprised how turning the scenario around like this can help to give us clarity when we can't see the woods for the trees.

Column 1 'WHAT' WHAT IT IS THAT SCARES ME?	Column 2 'WHY' WHY DOES IT SCARE ME?	Column 3 PUT THE FEAR INTO PERSPECTIVE	Column 4
I want to do a dressage test but am too scared to try	I will look silly if it goes wrong or I mess something up I should be doing better than I am I have been riding years! I dare not even try, the thought turns me to jelly! I don't believe I can do it My horse is green so he might play up half way through the test I feel inadequate I am not as good or experienced as other competitors I am afraid to try in case I forget the next move I can never get the correct diagonal (!)	Why? Who will think you are silly? Does it matter, it's just a bit of fun? We all have to start somewhere. Allowing peer pressure to get you down? Why do you worry what others think? All horses have to have a first time, why not just accept that and go for it? You have as much right to try as anyone else. Have a caller read the test for you as backup? It doesn't matter, one mistake is not the end of the world. Just go and	

		My horse is not as athletic or advanced as the others so I may not look good enough	have a try, enjoy it.	
		What if I have a melt-down and want to leave the arena half way through	Chances are, once you are in there you will see it through but if you want to leave you can.	
		People will make fun of me as I have no experience	Can you downgrade a level or do a simpler test for the first few times?	
		I don't have the latest clothing or smart, expensive tack.	Just look smart and turn your horse out well, that is all that matters.	

Column 4 - The Master Plan, working with your findings

In column 4 you can look at ways to rectify issues highlighted in the previous three. Once you have investigated the cause of the fear and looked at what it is about that particular aspect of competing that worries you, you will be able to start formulating a plan for conquering it. You can also use the ideas outlined in the previous chapters to break down training or competing into smaller 'bite-size' chunks and scoping out venues etc to prepare yourself.

Below are common examples of column 4 guidance but the basic content can be adapted to your personal situation (anxieties). This is the master plan, the recipe for breaking the barriers holding you back and allowing you to move forwards. Like all things where you have become stuck in a rut or feel like you have come up against a brick wall, it will take time to unravel but keep with it and you will be amazed how little steps become enormous leaps when you look back in a few months' time. Those entry forms will be completed and the rosettes will come. Just stick with the plans and refer to them whenever you need support.

I will look silly. Think about this. Will you really look silly? Who will think you are silly? Why does it matter to you if someone at the show thinks you can't perform as well as them? Why are they better than you (if they are)? Have they had lots of lessons or own a more experienced or more athletic horse? Is it a fact that their horse is very honest and they can go round the arena and 'get away with it' rather than because they have any great skill? I have seen many average riders take a placid, well-trained, honest horse into a dressage test or around a course of jumps. To the spectator they may appear amazingly talented. However, I have also seen it when these same riders try to get a difficult, young or unschooled horse around the same - often with varying success and certainly it didn't look as pretty as when they were on their schoolmaster! Anyone can look good on a good horse. Looking good (or at least looking like you are happy, confident and in control) on a naughty, green, young or unschooled one is the tricky part.

People can have a great social media following or do amazing things that you wouldn't perhaps want to tackle, but we all have our Achilles Heel. What I am trying to say is we all have our strengths and weaknesses so don't let others try to put you down or stop you. They may have a fierce reputation that goes before them, or be the local 'hero' but you, yes, little old you, have as much right as anyone to enjoy your horse and compete as they do. Don't let bullies put you off either, go out there with your head held high. It is easy to appear talented when the odds are in your favour but to me, the braver and often better rider is the one who is either slightly fearful but has a go anyway, and/or is on a tricky horse doing their best to get out to competitions. Perhaps it doesn't look too pretty in the early days but with time and practice it will improve so go and chase those rosettes!

What people have to realise is that if you watch the progress of a genuinely good rider over a period of time, you will see the horse progressing and learning properly. Respect should be given to a person who is keen and enthusiastic as a rider but maybe not, yet, as good in terms of skill as they would like but making every effort to have good tuition or improve themselves gradually with correct progressive training and getting out there at shows to enjoy their horse. It is not about looking silly, but positively addressing your current skill level, working on your shortcomings and ironing out these creases to strive to improve over time, which of course you will. Filling holes in our skillset is something that all top riders will see as ongoing. There is always someone better or more experienced and there is always the aim of perfection but don't let that worry you enough to stop you having a go.

Do not be afraid to hold your hands up and say "I am a bit wary about competing" but I am going to fix this with a positive attitude, taking my time, having a go, listening to what the judge has to say, striving to improve each time I go out and enjoying myself on my lovely horse because he and I are worth it! There is no shame in having lessons and listening to good advice. If you think you look silly because you are trying to do more than you or your horse is capable of at this time then the same applies, try to break it down into smaller steps, downgrade a level or pick a smaller show/venue to get you going or get you back in the swing of it after a break. Dig deep, soul search, try to find the real reasons. Then you can formulate your master plan for escaping the negative 'trap' you have fallen in to.

I should be doing better than I am. Beating yourself up mentally only means you become stuck in a cycle of upset and negativity because you feel down in the dumps about what you are currently achieving. Worrying and stressing because you want to be doing better than you are is not going to get you anywhere. You will improve by 'doing' and by improving your outlook, managing your expectations and re-training your mind-set. If the problem is one thing, then it is always worth seeing the solution as a slice in a pie – many slices making the whole, what I would call a multi-faceted approach. The slices of pie (the solutions) outnumber and overwhelm the one problem. For example:

1) Bite-sized 'learning and doing' chunks. Small steps, over time with patience, end up becoming big leaps and good progress. Look forward not backwards. Feel proud of any progression, however small it may be. Start small, end big!
2) Good, traditional instructors (emphasis on the word 'good') can be key to helping you improve in a safe way and achieve more than you ever thought possible. Listen to them and ask them specifically to assist you to do your personal show, tackle the cross-country element of the eventing or help you improve your jumping, practice the dressage test or whatever it is.
3) Riding a suitable mount, or a horse you are prepared to work with come good or bad days, for the type of element you are working at. As the old saying goes: 'horses for courses.'
4) Stop worrying what others think, comparing yourself at the yard, at the show or on social media and concentrate on being happy with your current situation (acceptance) and knowing that with hard work and determination you can move forward to a higher level (ambition and progression) if that is what you want to do.
5) Have the patience to work on the skills required for the job you are trying to undertake. Recognise your ability as a rider along with the capability of your horse. This is a very important step in successfully managing your fears and expectations. If you are sensible, and the situation is handled correctly, it will lead to fewer, and most importantly, manageable nerves. You will have the 'normal' nerves of a person who cares about what they are doing and wants to succeed but they will not be the crippling type with horrible physical side effects (increased heart rate, nausea, inability to think 'straight', dry mouth etc). Again, start small and progress to bigger venues/events if you want.

Also, think about the benchmark. Did you set it? Is it someone else's standard and actually, deep down you don't really want to do the same as them, or is it a genuine goal that you are determined to achieve? This is a big question because it is so easy to get drawn in to what we think we want because we are exposed to it rather than doing what we actually want. If you are trying to do more than you actually want to, no wonder you are uncomfortable. Really think about this factor. As I explained earlier, there is nothing wrong with some butterflies in the stomach before a competition, any sports person is bound to have these but they should not be debilitating. With strategic planning and mindfulness practice (we will come to that later) they can be managed and turned in to something positive. Believe it or not, you can turn these stomach churning nerves in to competitive edge, excitement and learn to use these feelings to sharpen your game as it were. Do what makes you happy. What is wrong with Intro or first level competition dressage if it makes you feel in control and capable? You can progress if you want to later. Who cares except you? Are you thinking because you have ridden for many years you should be more competitive and be hungry for trophies? Are you thinking this because you 'did it as a child' so you should do it now? Break it down into the feelings that affect **you** and try to look at them individually using the list you have already compiled and then apply the master plan for getting yourself started on the road to rectifying the issues. Acceptance of who we are and what we want are the first stages to overcoming our nerves, overcoming things in our heads that are physically holding us back.

We shall explore many helpful techniques as we go through the book, for example, trigger points, mindfulness or visualisation (explained fully later on) to help overcome anxiety and prep for an event. The self-analysis lists in the workbook are incredibly powerful, but must be used alongside hard work and hours in the saddle. You must be realistic about rectifying and overcoming your problems, sadly they will not usually just go away, you have to address them, understand them and work hard to rectify them and this does take time. It is not possible for everyone to ride every day and we should remember not to over-train. Both we and our horses need time out to rest and recuperate, but ride and do your emotional training as much as is practicably possible and always as well as you can. Keep at it. When something becomes second nature it becomes easier and that will shine through in competitions.

Today you may be feeling out of your depth, but things change and this does not have to be a forever situation. If you are not progressing consider if it is you, the horse, the game plan or the instructor which needs to change. You will need to take a step back to evaluate this from an honest perspective. It would be too easy to blame the instructor or the horse and quite often it is we who are at fault and not them. If you are determined to ride well and compete without fear you would be wise to have help, at least in the early stages, to get you going. A friend on the ground is fine if you are reasonably competent and just need some support or, perhaps, if there are financial constraints, but do not under estimate the progress you can make with the right set of tools.

It is entirely up to you but really and truly, if any elements of this book have made you realise you need to improve before you go out to compete, do try to find the funds for a lesson each week with a suitable instructor. They should give you homework so when your next lesson comes around, you have had things to work on and improve. They can work with you to achieve your goals and carefully set new ones which will in turn set you up for doing well in the show/event you want to attend.

If you are already a competent rider and the nerves are in no way down to skill (as I said, nervous doesn't always mean novice) then you are very lucky in some ways as you have the skills to back up your dreams. For you, it will be a case of methodically working through the lists with the self-analysis to find out what has gone wrong to change you from a happy competitor to a reluctant one, as well as doing the mindfulness work which we will come to later. Even if you think you know the answer to the cause of your anxiety, it is extremely important that you work through the lists to ensure you haven't missed any underlying issues which may be causing you worries but had until now remained unidentified.

A rider who is experienced and expected to do very well might feel considerable anxiety. There can be the feeling of immense pressure to perform and do well when one is held in high esteem or considered 'good' by others. When success is expected, it is actually intended to be a huge compliment but can feel so intense that it causes problems in itself. It certainly isn't down to a skills deficit or the lack of a trained horse, so from where does this kind of anxiety sneak its way in to our heads? When a certain level is accomplished, people will expect results and even staunch supporters and true friends will take the attitude that you will do well. This can actually be quite daunting and overwhelming. It is as if because you "win a lot" people think you don't have any worries or self-doubt and that you don't feel any stress at all.

I dare not do it at all. Why? Let's think about it. Does it correspond to the previous points? Maybe you dare not do it because social media floods us with people jumping bareback over enormous fences or you see 8 –year-old kids at the yard jumping 1 m 20 cm on a pony and feel that as an adult you are in some way inadequate. It is not so much inadequacy at this time in the journey, you are simply human and emotionally currently unable to complete the task you dream of. Take the pressure away from yourself with bite-sized chunks of progression.

Fill column 4 with your plans. Make them achievable and although your end result may be a 20-mile endurance ride, jumping the wings or competing at Grand Prix dressage, take it slowly and pay attention to not moving up a level until you feel relaxed at the one you are at. You almost, dare I say it, want to find your current level almost too easy and no longer a challenge. Then you will definitely be ready to go up a level and can keep doing so until you reach your target. It will take time so don't pressure yourself but have goals that you are sticking to and can realistically work with. You will be amazed how quickly that first show or test becomes going out every month with keen anticipation and actually enjoying yourself!

- **There will be scary things at the showground** or the horse won't like the white boards, big bright fillers, rustic fences etc. OK, so are these scary to you or to the horse? Are you making him fear something because you think he won't like it? If you are tense and he is looking to you to take him past/over things and you are not achieving that at present then you need to re-group, imagine yourself riding forward and positively past/over scary things whilst not over thinking or judging yourself.

By this time next year who knows what you will have achieved. Just don't fall in to the trap that someone else's limit is the same as yours and avoid setting your benchmark based on them. Their competence level may be less than yours in other areas but if it is currently greater than yours and their horse more schooled or physically able than yours at this time then that is fine, don't judge yourself. Just know where you are at now and formulate a plan to move on at your own pace, towards YOUR goals. You will get to that show and you will enjoy it, don't lose sight of it and don't fear the journey leading up to it. Believe you can and you will.

LOOKING AT YOUR FINDINGS AND WORKING WITH THEM

Having compiled, assessed and evaluated all the columns, you should now be in a position to understand your feelings and to have revealed the cause of those feelings. You can then formulate a plan of how to progress so that the fear does not win in the long term. Most fears can be approached in the same way as the example if you follow the plan and break it down. You must remain mindful of the competence/confidence equation as well as accepting that although you have identified the issues concerning you, it will take some time to overcome the negative feelings completely. Once you have found that balance, come to terms with it and accepted the associated feelings, you will find the way forward.

We now want to look at further ways to break down the negative blockages. For example 'I am scared of competing in case I can't remember the course' or whatever it is you have written has been broken down in the lists you have made. You have now hopefully opened your mind and your heart to the real causes of the fear so you can understand where it stems from and start to build up your confidence and mend your mind-set. We will assume at this stage that the fear is not because your horse is too much for your skill level and it is either:

1) a 'no good reason' fear that has crept up and you have no idea where it came from but you are suffering because of it;
2) a fear because you had a moment where things didn't go to plan and it's now playing on your mind and worrying you;
3) a fear stopping you from doing what you want to do because you haven't done it before or not done it for a long time and it worries you;
4) because you had an incident in the past which haunts you.

We must now look further at breaking down the issues so that they don't seem so daunting.

For example, earlier I described a gradual approach to entering a class or show, starting from watching others compete, sussing out the venue and then entering a class that is less than you are capable of in order to gain confidence. Whatever happens, don't allow yourself to get fixated with the issue as it will become 'bigger than it really is' in your mind and will not only upset you, but could, if you are tense, worry the horse which will lead to more problems. Try to keep everything in perspective.

If we assume that the horse and rider are both physically capable of doing their chosen discipline we can now look in detail at how to conquer fear in a structured format. You have identified and recognised the cause in your workbook so now you can rationalise it and deal with it. With the knowledge and self-acceptance of your current situation, you can now put the measures described in place to tackle the anxiety so that progression will come naturally and your fear will fade.

There are some techniques which you can do at home to strengthen your mind-set further. Easy to follow visualisation techniques and reflexology points to help back up all the hard world you are doing with your lists and self-discovery. These tools are great for strengthening resolve and every time you use them, done properly, you will see that they result in you becoming calmer and more confident each time you compete.

PRACTICAL TECHNIQUES TO CONQUER ANXIETY

Some other strategies to use alongside your workbook

The brain does not cope well with negatives. The human mind, evolved to rationalise, assess and act in different situations can become overloaded, resulting in negative experiences and feelings snowballing out of control. The key is to slowly turn the negatives into positives. Although we still have to think about the confidence/competence equation and take responsibility for our physical training, the mind can be helped to spring clean and clear out its negative storage areas with a number of positive mindfulness techniques. See the diagrams on the next page to see how negatives and positives can breed more of the same type of thoughts and become your general mind-set. This is great for positives but debilitating for those stuck in the negative cycle.

As you will see from the following simplified diagrams, the 'snowball' effect makes the initial feelings or mind-set grow and grow like a vicious circle. Emotions can get out of control and the growing negative thoughts, can leave you feeling terribly inadequate with no self-worth, low self-esteem and feeling like a failure.

You need to break the cycle and let the positive thoughts grow and snowball which in turn will lead to a happier, more positive you! It's true that positivity grows into more positivity, so try to remember this when times are hard and things are not going your way. No emotion has to be forever, so use mindfulness and positive visualisation to help change your outlook whenever you can. We will explore these useful techniques next.

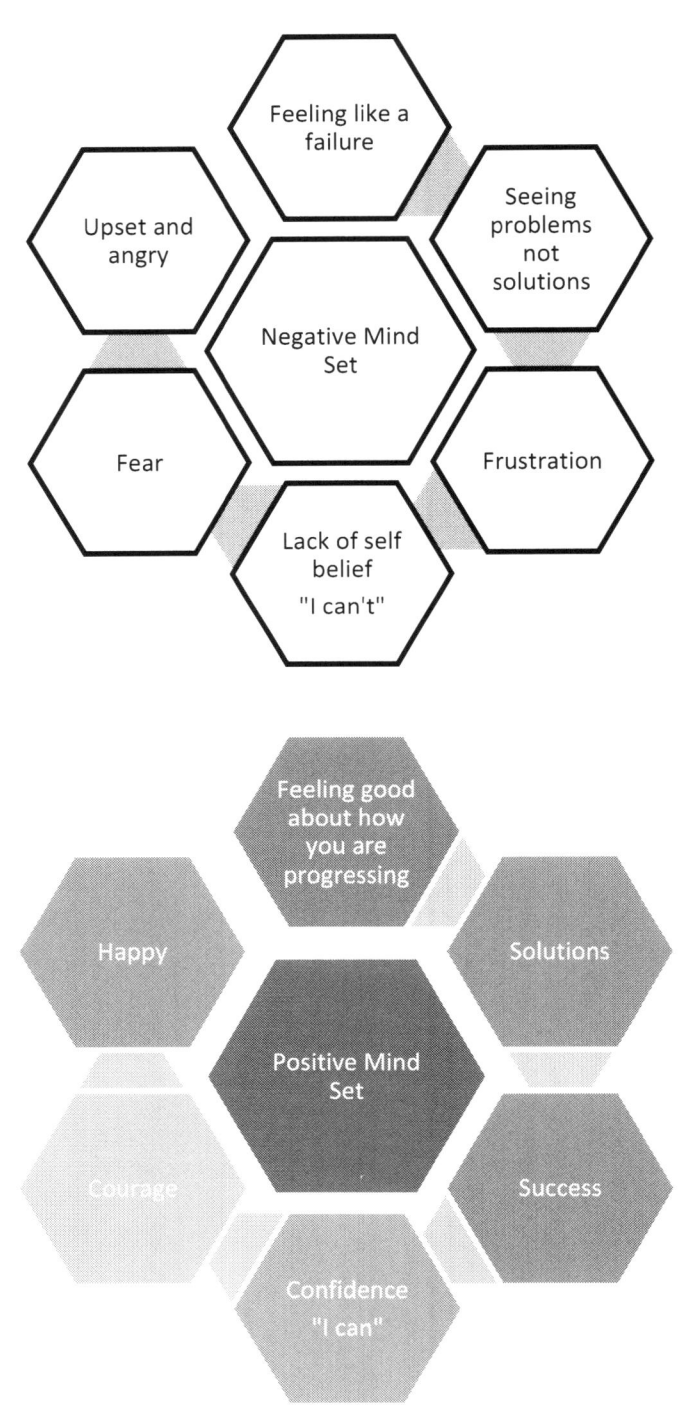

Dealing with anxiety emotionally and physically at the same time is the best way of getting over it. We want our fears to be forgotten so that we can move on to a fun, exciting and hopefully fulfilling future competing. We are going to explore ways to enhance the 'recovery' process with powerful techniques which are excellent tools and should not be overlooked, especially useful after you have identified the cause of the fears by using the workbook and have formulated a physical plan for moving forward with your goals. When you reach this stage of the programme, you can look at more ways to further squash the anxiety and manage your feelings towards competition.

Deep Breathing and Reflexology

I was shown a brilliant technique and continue to have fantastic results by putting a physical point on my body. In my case, I hold my thumb and say a trigger word while breathing deeply. This controls my pre-competition anxiety and channels my energy in such a way that I am able to focus clearly on what I have to do once in the arena. I was regularly competing and had dealt with my fears really well and actually felt very positive about competition, which was a great achievement in itself but I still wanted to take it further. As a result of using my workbook, which had uncovered the hidden root of my fears and given me the strength to formulate a plan to get out there in the arena, I felt very much in control with just the normal excited 'butterflies' one would expect before performing. However, I wanted to progress further and felt I needed to fine-tune my mind further.

I know that breathing may be something we do all the time but deep breathing is different. If you're not sure where to start, there is something known as 'four count' breathing. Simply place one hand on your tummy to encourage deep breathing, inhale to a count of four, then exhale for a count of four while imagining that you're drawing the first of four lines of a square. After pausing for two counts, you'll repeat that breathing sequence another three times to complete your square. You can then repeat the whole process a few times to focus and quieten your mind, concentrating only on your inhalation and exhalation. If you are breathing deeply, you will feel your hand rising and falling with your breath. I did it before going to bed a couple of nights a week and, with practice, I learned to be confident using the technique so I could call on it prior to competing or during any stressful situation where I needed to calm myself down. We hear it said all the time "Just breathe," but it's not very useful if you don't practise it before the stressful situation. When people get anxious and say "Oh I'm going to do deep breathing", it's probably not going to help very much unless it is something they have worked at and developed beforehand. Breathing is a very powerful tool but if you have never practised it before, it will be difficult to use it to any great effect for an instant fix of calm in times of stress as it needs to be developed to fully benefit from it.

Once you can do the 'square' and breathe deeply to whatever degree you can manage, it will have a positive effect and each time you use the technique, you are under-pinning a physiological response that you can reach for when you need it. Having learned to use the 'square' deep breathing and using my thumb as a trigger, in no time at all, as soon as I held my thumb in the certain way, said or thought the trigger word (in my case it was 'success') I could feel my heart rate drop, relaxation wash over me and my game went from zero to hero! I had successfully managed most of the problem by doing the visualisations and lists which were the biggest part of turning the fear around, but as I wanted to compete at a higher level, I decided to take matters further and work on improving my competition mind which certainly helped me use the pre-performance nerves to my advantage by turning them into a cool, collected, calm response with the 'trigger'.

The trigger technique enabled me to start enjoying competing even more than I was. Now I felt ready for anything. I also learned that rather than trying to get rid of the nerves completely, it's more helpful to prepare for them and figure out how to perform with some nerves. Manageable levels of nerves that are under control can enhance your game, not ruin it. Indeed, through practice with deep, slow breathing and holding my thumb, I now have a 'quick fix' before competition and so can you, provided you practice it regularly before you need it.

Before every competition I have the same routine. I sit for a minute in the horsebox or anywhere I can have a private few minutes (yes, even in the loo). I shut my eyes and try to focus. I start the process of taking big, deep diaphragmatic breaths, holding them for a second and exhaling. After a few, I take my thumb in my other my hand and as I exhale I say the word "success" either out loud or in my head if it is not possible to speak at volume. I repeat this a couple of times. This technique works every time, it reduces my anxiety and completely calms me down. It allows me to concentrate and is a game changer as I feel ready for the competition and able to face whatever is happening in a calm, confident, rational way.

You don't have to use the same 'point' as me or say the same word, you can choose whatever you want, but I recommend using any known reflexology point and a positive, simple word such as 'success', 'win', 'achieve' or similar. Once you get in to the swing of this, you will be absolutely amazed how much this changes your outlook. You must practise it regularly in order to use it successfully before every competition but if you do, it will help you be as good as you can be. Even though I was feeling pretty good about riding, the benefit of fine tuning really enabled me to 'up my game' and taught me how to control my emotions to an even greater degree as well as work on controlling the 'good' competition nerves and using them for competitive edge rather than associating them with horror. Without doubt, my results and scores went through the roof as a result of knowing how to handle the nerves and channel the energy I had into something constructive that would help rather than hinder me.

When I chose the thumb I had no prior knowledge that it was a known reflexology point. I found this very interesting when I later looked it up and saw that it was associated with calming oneself. I went with my instinct because it felt 'right,' which maybe signifies that sometimes our subconscious or our body knows best. Reflexology teaches that the thumb is responsible for anxiety (and headaches). If you're experiencing nerves (or a nervous headache), hold your thumb for about five minutes. Reflexologists say it will relieve the symptoms and calm you down. This has certainly been the case for me although I do use it with the deep breathing at the same time as well as saying my 'trigger' word.

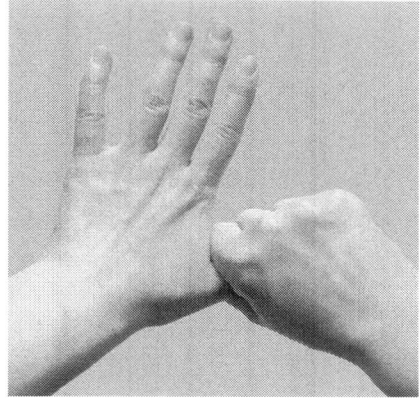

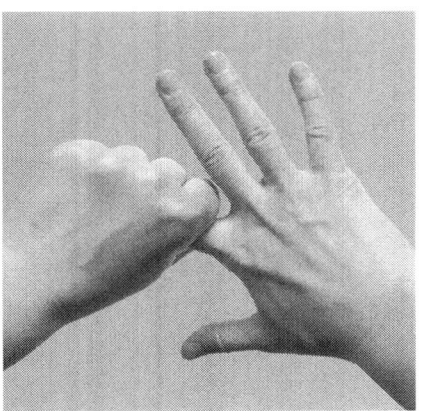

Another good trigger point may be the fore finger. It is believed that this finger controls muscle pains as well as feelings of disappointment, fear and embarrassment.

The little finger is responsible for self-esteem, stress, and nervousness. If you're prone to diminishing your worth, you should really think about massaging it for five minutes. Try to think of something nice or perhaps doing well in competition, while doing it.

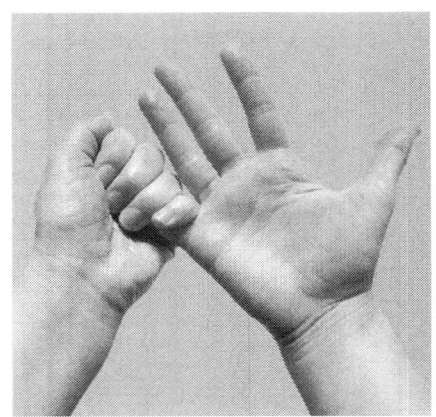

Negative emotions and sadness will go away if you softly clutch your ring finger for five minutes. Don't forget to concentrate on your breathing and use your trigger word if that appeals to you as a technique.

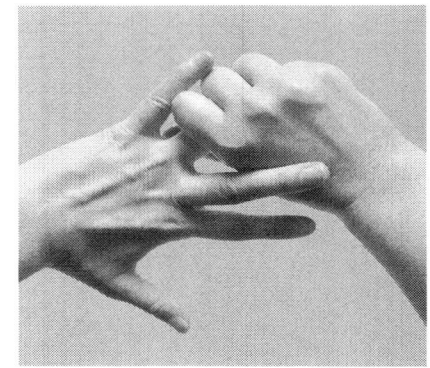

Mindfulness – Positive Visualisation

Anxiety tends to crop up in stressful situations with uncertain outcomes. The already present stress of competition gets exacerbated by the fact that you just don't know how it's going to turn out. You might find yourself running through every single terrifying possibility in your head, irrespective of whether you can do anything about it. Unfortunately, those outcomes aren't usually things you have the final say on, that is for the judge or 'luck on the day,' whether there is a loud bang in the car park just as you go up the centre line or whether you knock a pole down etc. You only really have control over yourself, which is why we practice mindfulness techniques to learn to cope and be as in control of our minds as possible. We have to rationalise our thoughts towards competing, asking "Is this something that I have control over? If not, what is it that I do have control over, and how do I place my focus on that?" So, when anxious thoughts are snowballing, try to acknowledge that some of your fear is coming from the uncertainty of the situation, and spend your energy working on the things you *can* control. I like to work with visualisation to do this and I will take you through how to do that now.

Choose a quiet time. When you go to bed is ideal as you can do your visualisation before you sleep, allowing your brain to process the scenario overnight and without interruption. Visualisation is great because not only is it free, you can do it yourself and fit it in around your life. You do not have to be a guru or an expert to do this, just sit back and give it a go, have faith in yourself to see it through. You may be wary about trying visualisation but you will be amazed how quickly your mind becomes accustomed to the visualisation process and you will soon learn to do it and enjoy it, most importantly, without any negatives creeping in.

First, pick the scenario that worries you, i.e. the show, event, course etc. Then imagine riding that event by closing your eyes and imagining it in detail. This must be a calm, positive, happy and nice scenario, in a place you feel drawn to, whether you have been there in real life or intend to go in the future, e.g. a show ground, an arena or cross country course, somewhere you intend to compete when you are ready. You remember we looked at going for a recce? In visualisation, having done this, you can more easily imagine that place in detail which will give you a very strong foundation from which to build your perfect 'story'.

The visualisation can be for as much time as you feel appropriate, there is no right or wrong so just go with what works for you. It is important whilst practicing the meditation that you are not judging yourself, just witnessing and moving on a positive journey. You could even write the 'story' down, record it on your phone and play it back to ease the creative process if you struggle doing the visualisation from scratch although I think if you concentrate you will be surprised how easy it is to do this kind of technique. However you proceed, take time to describe or imagine your 'story' in detail and ensure you do not rush.

Here is a brief example to get you started. I have condensed it but in reality, you should add as much detail as you want to and tailor it to match what you will be doing and the format it will take. The visualisation should always be your own as the most important thing is to take into account your issues or worries:

Imagine arriving at the stables, grooming and loading up ready for the show/event. You feel calm and happy as you prepare your beautiful horse for travelling. You feel good that you are going out. Excited, but essentially very calm, you feel in control as you know your horse is in tiptop condition and you will look amazing when you arrive. Visualise yourself travelling safely to the venue, unloading, entering the secretary's office to collect your number and tacking up. You are relaxed and have plenty of time before your class will be called. You feel full of excitement but incredibly calm, really in control and eager to compete. You know you are capable and this is your chance to shine. It is a beautiful day and your horse's coat is gleaming. Your show gear is immaculate and you are changed and ready to go to the warm-up area/collecting ring. You know you both look lovely. You feel ready to compete. You are a good rider and you have a good horse. You check your tack, mount and walk over to the warm-up area. You feel proud of yourself and proud of your horse. You are both relaxed and in the warm up he moves beautifully. He is listening to you and being well-behaved. You feel confident and full of happiness. The other competitors are in the collecting ring, you are not concerned by them and when your class is called you are able to walk in with an air of purpose and confidence. You know you can do this. You are happy, your horse is happy, you know it will go well and you are confident of placing highly. You can hear your horse's gentle breathing as you go forward to perform. You ride beautifully in the group and the judge calls you in to the first line up, you are in first place. You feel amazing but still calm. Your personal show goes perfectly, you and your horse go round effortlessly, all your hard work has paid off and you are doing the best you can do. The judge is smiling, you are a pleasure for them to watch. You are enjoying your ride and you feel confident you are doing well. You complete your ride. The judge is smiling so you know you are on top form. The steward beckons you in to the final line-up. You feel amazing. You have done it, you have won! The judge clips a beautiful red rosette to your horse's bridle. You are elated and are smiling proudly. You have successfully competed and the judge motions for you to lead the lap of honour. You are still calm but smiling uncontrollably. You canter round and the crowd claps. You come back to a walk to leave the arena. You nod to the judge and say thank you. You feel ecstatic, it has all gone amazingly well. You feel on top of the world and your smile is as big as it can possibly be. You pat your horse and walk confidently back to the horsebox with your rosette pinned to his bridle. You have done brilliantly. You have placed well and are thrilled. The birds are singing, it is bright and warm, you are so happy and proud, and it is a perfect day. The horse is walking along gently and calmly, he knows he has done well too. You are both at one, enjoying your time together, everything is safe and well, you are happy and full of enjoyment. You go back to the horsebox, untack and take time to offer your horse a drink. You put the tack away and load him on to the box and drive him home safely. The feeling is amazing, you arrive home at the yard and tell your friends how great it was and how you can't wait to go to the next one! YOU are a competitor, a successful competitor, full of confidence, ability and loving it!

Be sure in this scenario that you don't let any doubts creep in, that there is nothing to scare or concern you and you are so happy, just enjoying the sensation of riding in your competition. Let it play out like a movie in your mind's eye. Always go full circle, from start to finish, conclude your scenario by visualising you both going home to the yard, washing him off or grooming him and putting him in the field or stable so that the day is complete and you feel in control. The visualisation must be complete from going out to coming home, all the time remaining happy, positive, calm and safe.

You can make this fit your fear, so for example if the warm up ring bothers you, tailor your scenario in to a beautiful day with a fun, relaxing time in a quiet warm up where you are happy and in control, ready and set for your class. If the class worries you, visualise the perfect ride and always focus on a good outcome, it doesn't mean that you will always come first, but certainly, there is no harm visualising that you do. As they say, reach for the stars...

Each time you do the visualisation (I recommend daily) really feel what you are 'seeing'. Ride every detail of your show, course or event in your head so that when you come to do it for real it goes like clockwork and you will be surprised how the actual event reflects the visualisation. I always think if the preparation is done this way, it is almost like you have ridden it before. When you first do this to prepare yourself for an event, I would certainly do the visualisation for as long as you have got. If you need to compete in a four weeks' time, start now. Don't leave it until the night before to start. Preparation is key. If you only have a few days or a week, I would suggest starting as soon as you can and do the exercise daily leading up to your event taking place, especially the night before. I cannot stress enough how much the visualisation in the beginning must ALWAYS be a positive, calming one in which you and your horse enjoy yourselves and you feel love, excitement and joy as you are riding in your particular scenario. Mindfulness or visualisation doesn't necessarily have to mean the traditional idea of meditation. I like to do it at night but you can work with it how you want and if it means you are out walking or in your lunch-break at work, go for it.

It is widely recognised that visualising an ideal outcome over and over again to create a mind-set of success is without doubt effective and for most people will be all they need to do. However, there is a school of thought that once you are at a more advanced level and looking to iron out even more creases, you can work at visualising challenging, unexpected or difficult scenarios where challenges are thrown at you but you ride through them and cope easily with the unexpected. I don't recommend this for beginning visualisation but some sports coaches would certainly employ this alongside the 'perfect' scenario. For example, visualising riding in bad weather, missing a stride or taking the wrong canter lead or whatever, can be a way of coping if these things occur. You are still riding to win, literally committed to doing your best and giving 100% but having visualised how you would cope if these things arose, so when in reality you come up against a challenging moment, you can say "I've got this, my horse can be controlled, I can come back from the mistake. I am competent and I have corrected this a million times before. It will not upset the rest of my ride and I am still able to continue, un-flustered and un-hindered."

You are practising how you'll respond to tough situations to prove to yourself that you can survive the worst, if it should happen. You are coming to terms with the uncertainties and walking yourself through hypothetical, 'what if' situations which should help you feel like you have more control. Also, if something does go wrong, chances are it will far more likely be something smaller than the utter doom you imagined, like downing a pole or missing a canter stride or lead change. It won't be totally new terrain and you'll know you can get through it, even if it's unpleasant.

I find I don't need to work with the negatives, I only use the positive visualisation but not to give you the two options would be unfair. You can choose whichever way of handling it you think is best, but if you are nervous or reluctant to compete anyway, whether you have done so before or not, I would certainly always do the positive scenario before you tackle the 'what if' visualisations. If you do want to go further as you improve in competition and start to look at the 'what if'' strategies, maybe that is a task for a few years down the line and I urge caution here as you do not want to accidentally put more dread in to your already overloaded mind.

Whatever type of visualisation you choose to try, go with what works for you and do the best you can. If your mind drifts, get back on track as soon as it does. Pick up the visualisation where you were at the point you lost concentration and carry on. Within a few days you will be able to play the scene out in your mind without too much difficulty. If you fall asleep it doesn't matter, your subconscious mind is still working and taking all the information on board. Also, don't think because it is a competition that you have to feel aggressive or bullish. In fact, the calmer and more laid back you are, the better the outcome. If you visualise being het-up that is not what you are trying to achieve. The natural on the day adrenalin will notch you up enough for a good performance so bring it all together and quieten things down as this will serve you well in the long term.

Kinesiology

Another powerful tool to consider is Kinesiology. The study of mental issues and blocks as well as physical performance, emotional function and all round wellbeing. A qualified Kinesiologist will use a non-invasive system of muscle response testing to identify and eliminate mental and physical problems. It is probably more associated with allergy testing but Kinesiology is a powerful tool for helping you re-set your mental and physical balance which in competitive sport is a great tool as it will allow you to feel more in control and able to perform at your very best.

It is purported that people can benefit from Kinesiology in a number of ways, including:

Enhanced learning abilities.
Improved sports performance.
Eliminating emotional, physical and mental stress in general or for individual issues.
Assisting with decision-making.
Overcoming past trauma.
Identifying nutritional excess or deficiency.
Aiding in muscle injury healing.
Releasing fears and phobias, giving you the courage to move on.

I have used Kinesiology for a number of years and it has definitely enhanced my well-being on many occasions. I have successfully cleared emotional blockages and it has helped me with confidence, stress, diet and nutrition and identified a number of health issues which, although minor, have been dealt with to avoid complications in the future. I would recommend this to anyone who is in need of a boost and if you want to use it to help with your competitive performance, just discuss this with the practitioner who will know how to assist you. Kinesiology works extremely well with our lists and EFT tapping (see next page) so all these processes combined can help you achieve your goals, especially when you have worked so hard to iron out many of the creases by yourself but still have a minor blockage that you need help to overcome. Many Progressive Kinesiologists will use EFT Tapping so if you are unsure, maybe book a single session so they can guide you initially. Everyone will teach their own method but do what feels right and works for you.

Emotional Freedom Technique/Tapping

Writing down things that worry us is a well-known therapeutic method. Not only does this outline the fears in black and white but helps us on the way to processing the problem by 'seeing' it and deep down, helping to release the energy connected to this problem. A good, qualified Kinesiologist can work further with you on these matters if you would like to see a practitioner in person. However, you can do the Tapping element of this yourself at home. It is easy to do, absolutely free of charge and works brilliantly alongside our lists and positive mind-set visualisations. I have found this has helped many riders including myself.

Emotional Freedom Technique (EFT) is a form of psychological acupressure, based on the same energy meridians used in traditional acupuncture to treat physical and emotional problems but with no needles. In a nutshell it is a positive reprogramming technique where you tap on parts of your anatomy with your fingers while repeating aloud a phrase or 'mantra' and feeling how your emotions change during the course of the process.

It is believed this system works by tapping with the tips of the fingers to target the acupuncture points on the face and body where energy is getting stuck or stagnant in order to clear blockages. Energy traveling through these channels can once again flow freely throughout the physical body. It is also believed that doing this when looking in a mirror magnifies the effect. It is a strange feeling at first but the good thing is once you stop feeling self-conscious about sitting or standing there tapping yourself and saying your positive affirmation out loud, you can fit this in to the busiest lifestyle and reap the benefits.

There are many EFT articles out there for you to read but most seem to agree that when you have identified an issue, in this case fear of competing, you can tap out the blocked energy in a few easy steps. If you have more than one issue or fear, you can repeat this sequence to address each in turn to reduce or eliminate the intensity of your negative feeling. I would advise that you tackle one thing at a time for maximum effect, it is the same with lists and visualisation, focusing on one problem at a time is likely to enhance your outcome and not overload or overwhelm you.

Step 1 - Initial feelings on a scale of 1 to 10

Once you have successfully identified the area you want to work on rate it a level on a scale of 1 to 10 (1 being mild, 10 being intense worry). This initial assessment helps you see where you are on an emotional level and will give you something to work from in terms of reducing the intensity. For example, if your fear starts at ten but after using the tapping techniques you feel it has reduced to a seven or below it is a significant improvement. Over a period of time the level of intensity of the negative feeling should diminish meaning that the fear has been suitably dealt with and significantly diminished or, even better, it has been eradicated completely. Providing the competence/confidence equation has been addressed and is balanced, the tapping programme can help you reinforce your positive mind-set and help you break free from your emotional stresses to go forward in your competition life.

Step 2 - Setting up the positive affirmation or 'mantra'

So, you are ready to start working on the tapping, you have established your fear or issue and now you need to make up a simple phrase (mantra) that will help you acknowledge the fear and accept yourself despite the issue you are facing. The one I believe is a common setup phrase is: "Even though I (insert your fear or problem, e.g. cantering in the show ring), I deeply and completely love and accept myself anyway." After a couple of days of this, introduce a positive 'next step' mantra – something along the lines of "I will successfully compete and choose to enjoy (insert your fear, e.g. cantering in the show ring)." The mantra can be adapted to your exact requirements and can change over time as you progress mentally.

Step 3- The tapping sequence

The EFT tapping sequence is the methodical tapping of your fingers on the acupressure points. I usually tap five times at each point whilst saying my mantra. This teaches us to be in charge of our own mind and create our own outlook.

Although there are twelve meridians the EFT technique focuses on these nine. Begin by tapping the karate chop point on your hands while simultaneously reciting your mantra, then tap each following point five times with your finger-tips, moving through the points in this order:

- 'karate chop' your hand
- inner edge of eyebrow
- side of the eye
- under the eye in the centre

- under the nose in the centre
- chin in the centre
- just under the collarbone
- under the armpit
- finish on the top of the head in the centre

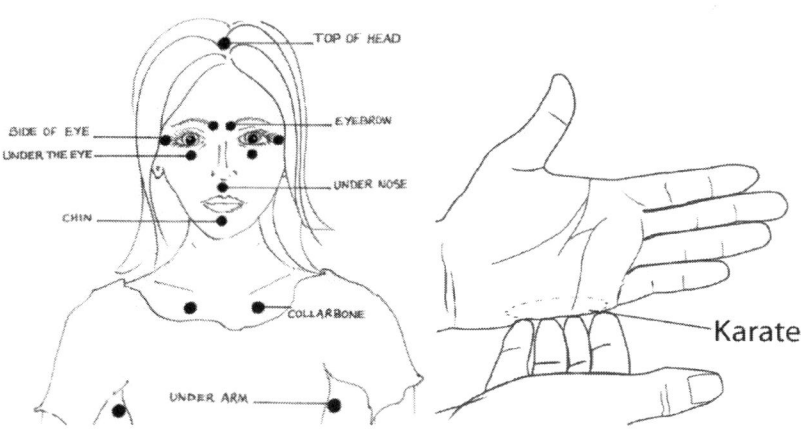

4. Rate your fear

After doing the tapping a few times, rate the intensity of the fear as you feel it now. Compare your results with your initial intensity level. If you haven't yet reached 0, repeat the process until you feel the intensity is lower than it was (of course 0 is ideal but I think any lower number is a step in the right direction). Keep at it until you are in the lower figures, let's say, hopefully in the 0 – 4 range. You will notice that over time the fear will subside but you do have to keep chipping away at it. Nothing worth having is easy or instant so don't give up just because it doesn't happen straight away.

This is a great technique for dealing with fears and worries and although at first it can feel slightly strange, is a powerful tool to have in your repertoire. I found that tapping two or three times a day worked well, but of course, do what feels right or suits you. Another tip is to write your positive affirmation on a sticky note and pin it to your mirror in the bedroom so you can read it before bed and when you get up. Take every opportunity you can to embed this positive mind-set in your life. Believe in what you are saying, you have to mean it for it to become reality although the tapping helps cement it.

HORMONES AND ANXIETY

This is worth consideration if you are suffering from anxiety that appears to have crept up on you out of nowhere or is affecting more than just your riding. It may be worth considering having a chat with your doctor to discuss whether your anxiety is linked to a hormonal imbalance. This can affect men and women although due to our constantly changing hormones, seems to affect females more frequently. I am not a doctor and not trying to be, so will not even start to dish out medical advice, but hormones can be tricky things and if there is an imbalance, it is worth having this investigated.

A hormonal imbalance can make you feel awful, jittery, uneasy and impact negatively on everyday life. This is not the same as the anxiety experienced before a show or in any situation with an uncertain outcome. This anxiety should not be ignored, but once identified can usually be treated easily, so don't worry. It is intense, persistent and seems constantly present but for no reason. You may find that you are having to 'talk yourself' into doing the simplest, everyday tasks and feel as if it is taking over your existence. Hormones fluctuate throughout a woman's life, but whether monthly, menopausal or during and after child birth they can be 'all over the place.' I have had women approach me wondering why they have gone from being nerve-free when riding to very anxious indeed 'for no reason'. The reason, generally speaking, is that their hormones have got a little out of balance and once steps have been taken to put things right they are fine again.

Our bodies are wonderful things, fine pieces of engineering, and like all machines need looking after (healthy diet and lifestyle) and servicing (health check-ups with the doctor). Despite our best efforts, they occasionally need to be fixed, so if you are feeling something isn't 'quite right', rather than allow the situation to worsen, it is sensible to get the problem investigated as soon as you can. Hormones are messengers, they affect all kinds of things: appetite, sleep, mood, behaviour and outlook to mention a few. We do need them, obviously. For example, adrenaline warns us of danger and, when the danger is gone, should automatically go back to a normal level. However, when they get out of balance they can be rather unhelpful and go a bit crazy, so definitely need to be stabilised. Although our hormone levels are always in a state of flux, there are scales or levels that are considered 'normal' and this is where the doctor comes in to check that yours are functioning correctly.

Whatever is making you unhappy, it is crucial to get to the bottom of it and if it is a hormone imbalance it might answer a lot of questions for you once you have identified and treated it. A simple blood test can determine the hormone levels in your body and the doctor can advise you and treat you if necessary. It is better to find out than keep putting it off, as being on edge the whole time is no way to live and needs to be addressed in order to restore peace and harmony in your everyday life, not to mention your riding and the enjoyment of it.

TRAINING TIPS

Work hard in silence, let success make the noise…

Although not intended as a training or riding instruction manual per se, I thought it may be helpful for the reluctant or novice competitor to have a starting point. I have therefore put together a short guide to give the rider some tips about the more known disciplines. I hope you can adapt some of the fundamental ideas of training to fit your particular horse sport and, of course, there are numerous books and articles available specifically for your discipline. One thing that I think is particularly noteworthy: we refer to riding 'disciplines' because discipline is what it takes to be good at anything. Discipline in our training, work ethic and consistency is what we need to succeed as well as a good mind-set and love for the sport in which we compete.

One very valuable tool is relaxation. Take a few deep breaths and relax your body before entering the arena. A tense rider will make a tense horse. Remember it is supposed to be fun. If you have chosen to work with the trigger points previously discussed, use them before you mount or enter the ring with the breathing techniques. Then, before you go in, touch your chosen trigger point and you will have an extra-calm start to your performance.

Cross-Country

A thrilling but tough discipline where you need a fit, able horse and rider and quick reactions to enable you to control your horse to cross varied terrain, not to mention the solid, quite unforgiving jumps. To ride your line, adjust and judge speed whilst maintaining your nerve, balance and keeping the horse in a good rhythm.

Watch other events before you enter if possible and use the course walk to your advantage. I know that some riders like to jog the course so they get an idea of how the jumps will come up at speed and get a feel for the ground or 'going.' No doubt having jogged between the fences you will feel the gradient of slopes and hills so may be more aware of how your horse will feel during the course. Know when to back off and when to push him on.

When you have walked the course and are happy with how it flows and how it feels, don't forget to warm up thoroughly as the horse will be expected to leave the starting box cantering. Injuries can occur very easily if the time has not been spent preparing him properly. The warm up gives you a chance to instil confidence in your horse. The practise jump (often a log or fairly straight forward rustic jump) will give you time to calm any nerves as well as settle him and get him moving out in front of your leg so he feels ready to tackle the course. During the warm-up, ride the jumps on both reins equally and once the horse feels smooth and ready, adjust the angle slightly to practise different approaches.

Always 'ride your line,' which really means stick to the route you want to use from jump to jump and try not to deviate from this. As you progress the 'line' will be fine-tuned and used to knock seconds off your time despite the size and technicality of the jumps increasing. If you are taking things very seriously, use your watch, but if you are just starting out, worry more about how you are riding than the time. Faster times will come so don't let it rule you so you start to panic and make mistakes.

By the time you make your way to the start box, you should both feel ready for the course ahead and can go out with confidence and conviction. Your horse will be trying his heart out for you during the competition so be a good leader and encourage and assist him to do his job. During a one day event, you will have already done the dressage and show jumping so the horse should be in a good mind-set for the cross country. With a three-day event you will have each part on a separate day but can still use the show jumping to ready him for the next phase.

When you are on the course, aim to adjust your stride in plenty of time before the jump (5 strides may be optimum) to give you time to adjust the shape of his body to cope with the demand of the fence. A rider needs to be balanced too so that the horse only has to worry about getting himself over safely without too much encumbrance from the rider. An efficient cross-country horse will know his job but you need to understand how to adjust his speed effectively and keep him in balance without letting him dictate. A young or less-experienced horse may not be keen so back off at the last minute, while a strong, very bold or forward ride may be pulling like a train, so try to keep everything smooth and controlled by using your position and the aids to communicate what you need. Your instructor should have covered this in detail at home but in general, teach your horse to recognise the cruising position between fences which allows him to work underneath you, the balancing position on approach to a fence and the away position to increase speed, most probably on landing after a jump to pick up speed before returning to the cruising position once again.

Another sage piece of advice I was offered is ride forward in to water but take the speed down a little so you can ride it positively once you are in the five stride zone. The horse will of course be slower and need more energy to move through water but get your approach right then push forward through it, remaining helpful to the horse both entering, through and out again.

Try to enjoy the course. It will test you and your horse, but with the correct, progressive training and applying the little tips and tricks we have covered in this book it should be a pleasant experience for both of you.

As with all disciplines, don't forget the suitable after-care of your horse. Be sure to cool him down and attend to washing, rugging and treating any (hopefully) minor cuts and scrapes as necessary. Never under-estimate cold water on legs and if you have access to a solarium pop him under it when you get home. If not, ensure you pay attention to his needs and take into account the temperature and weather so as not to make mistakes with his care and well-being. In any case, do your after-care planning in advance to ensure you have everything you need.

Cross country, with all the galloping and exertion creates a lot of sweat and will not only test you and your horse but also your tack, so do make sure everything is fit for purpose and clean at the outset. Check it again after use for damage or wear. It is absolutely essential that tack fits well in any discipline but with the movement of cross-country, problems with anything that does not fit correctly show up very quickly. Avoid hurting yourself or your horse with good quality tack (well looked after, second-hand tack can be good quality) that fits and is checked regularly by a qualified saddler and/or knowledgeable person. If you need advice on what tack and equipment to use that works well, ask the other competitors what and why they use a particular style or brand.

In-hand showing

This may be obvious, but before the show get your horse as clean as possible. It may be worth bathing manes and tails a couple of days before if you have to plait, so that the natural oil is present to stop them falling out. Practise what you will need to do before going in the ring. Practise running with your horse so he shows off his trot but doesn't canter unless he is supposed to, get your horse listening to you and very importantly, practise a nice square halt and standing still. Perhaps use a friend as a 'judge' who you can present your horse to.

In the class at the show the ring steward will let you in the ring. You are immediately on show so act accordingly. The horse will be on the right rein for most of the time with you leading him on the outside of the ring. This allows the judge the best view of your animal. Make him walk actively so you don't look like you are dragging him round but don't allow him to get too far in front of your shoulder so he looks as if (or indeed, does) run off with you. The judge will ask you to walk round the ring for what can seem like an eternity but don't pull faces, just professionally do as you are asked.

The steward will then stop you, usually in a queue in the corner of the ring. When you stop, allow space (at least one horse's length) between you and the competitor in front so you don't run the risk of getting kicked or, if the horse moves backwards, stood on. One by one you will be required to run with your horse in trot around half if not all of the arena. If you are not a good runner or feel you need a break, try not to stop until you are out of the line of sight of the judge. You will run to the back of the queue and can get your breath back while the others take their turn.

After the individual trot up in line, you will be asked to walk round the ring in line as a group again. At this point you will be pulled into a line up in the centre of the ring. Sometimes this is any old how, sometimes you will be pulled in in an initial order of favourites going from left to right. One by one the judge will ask you to bring you horse forward. You may be asked questions such as how old the horse is, breed and what you do with him. While the judge is asking questions get your horse standing square. This is where the judge will have a good look at his confirmation and get a good general impression close up.

When the judge has had a brief chat to you and seen enough, they will ask you to walk away from them, turning to the right at a set point (usually near the end of the ring) and then run (the horse will trot) in a straight line back towards them. You will run past them and then once you have turned the corner, can come back to a walk and re-join the line up in the place you came from. Always enter the line up from the back so you don't cut in front of anyone else. Once back in line, keep your horse standing square and keep him quiet. Do not be tempted to feed bits of grass you have picked if you are showing outdoors or mints from your pocket as you will only succeed in making the judge see that you are bribing the horse and that he is not mannerly enough to stand quietly without your interaction. Worst case scenario, you will teach him to nip or bite looking for food (not so good if it's the judge he nips) and he may learn to be restless and paw the ground to try and get attention for food, which is not a good way to show him off or teach him good manners.

When everyone has been judged individually you will then be asked to walk around the ring again while the judge makes their mind up. He or she will ask the steward to bring you in in the order of placing: the first competitor gets pulled in first and so on. Wherever you place, keep smiling, thank the judge and steward and don't be ungracious.

Ridden showing

Just the same as for in-hand showing, do get your horse as clean as possible. Don't use show shine or any product with silicon in it anywhere were tack goes. It will be very slippery and potentially dangerous. Do not saddle soap leather reins as they can become slippery. Practise what you will need to do before going in the ring. Practise riding your horse in the figure of eight show pattern as well as getting your horse listening to you and very importantly, practice a nice square halt and standing still. Perhaps use a friend as a 'judge' to whom you can present your horse.

The ring steward will let you in the ring so now you are in the spotlight. Act accordingly. As a group you will be asked to walk, trot, then canter on one rein, then as a group you will normally come back to trot, change rein, and canter on as a group again. Don't cut anyone up, but if the person in front is slower than you, it is generally deemed appropriate to pass them but in such a way that you are giving them space, not affecting anyone else in the ring and

not roaring past trying to cause a scene. The steward will ask the group to go back to walk and either will be told to line up in any order or pulled in initial places. If you are not pulled in in order, try to make your way to the middle of the group.

One by one the judge will ask you to bring you horse forward. You may be asked questions such as how old the horse is, breed and what you do with him. Politely give clear, concise answers. While the judge is asking questions keep your horse still and standing square as this is where the judge is getting a good close up look at him. When they've seen enough they will invite you to perform your individual show.

When everyone has been judged individually you may then be asked to walk around the ring again while the judge makes their mind up. Even if your personal show was not quite what you anticipated, keep riding properly and remain professional until the very end. The judge will pull you in in the order of placing, i.e. the winning competitor gets pulled in first and so on. After the placings, the top three will be asked to do a lap of honour. Usually before this takes place the other competitors will be invited to leave the ring. As you leave, if practical, either nod or thank the steward/judge as you file out or if you are lucky enough to be in the top three, wait in line to be asked to do your lap of honour. The lap of honour is supposed to be dignified and although you may gallop if confident, be mindful of other competitors and perhaps a beautiful canter is a safer and prettier option, but I will leave you to make that call on the day.

Show Jumping

Warm your horse up properly in the practise ring including jumping a couple of jumps as preparation. The warm-up gives you a chance to instil confidence in your horse and the practise jump will give you time to calm any nerves as well as settle him and get him moving so he feels ready to tackle the course. During the warm-up, ride the jumps on both reins and once the horse feels smooth and ready, adjust the angle slightly to practise different approaches. Always 'ride your line' which really means stick to the route you want to use from jump to jump and try not to deviate from it. As you progress the 'line' will be fine-tuned and used to knock seconds off your time despite the size and technicality of the jumps increasing, but for now stick to riding as well as you can and as calmly as you can.

Remember to pass left to left in the practise ring and let other competitors know when you are jumping a practise fence to avoid a crash. Walk the course as you are planning on riding it, remembering to check you know where the start and finish markers are and don't forget after the last jump that your round doesn't finish until you have gone through the finish markers. Watch a couple of competitors jump the course to see how it rides if you can. This will allow you to see how it rides in real time and despite your course walk, you will see if there is an element which seems to be catching everyone out so you can formulate a plan to approach it.

The steward will let you in the ring. Ride round and be sure to go past the judges so they can see your competitor number and you can give them a friendly smile or nod. Wait until the bell has rung indicating you can start your round. If you start before the bell you will be eliminated. Ensure you go through the start markers, these will vary from electronic beams to more basic 'start' signs pushed in the grass or standing on the arena surface. Look ahead, look at your next jump as soon as you can. Where you look you will generally go so this is a key part of successfully getting to the next jump smoothly. On completion of your round ensure you go through the finish markers before leaving the arena. Again, these will vary but make sure you don't forget to go through them. The elation of a clear, well-jumped round can make you lose focus, so don't make a rookie error and forget the easy part of completing the course.

This can vary but generally, once all the competitors have jumped their first round there will be a draw of all the clear rounds which will indicate the order of the jump off. The jump off is over a shortened, timed course so that the fastest clear round or fastest round with least faults wins. Some competitions will run as a two phase round. Once you have completed the first, untimed round, you will continue straight into the second which will be over the same course but timed. The second section faults and fastest time will determine the final placings. At the end of the class competitors who are placed will be invited into the ring to collect their rosettes and/or prizes. Whatever happens, keep smiling and remain gracious.

Dressage

Relax. Take a few deep breaths and relax your body before entering the arena. A tense rider will make a tense horse. Remember it is supposed to be fun. If you have chosen to work with the trigger points we discussed in the book, use them with the breathing before you mount, then before you go in, touch your chosen trigger and you will have an extra-calm approach. It is often said (and I would agree to a point) that it is not always wise to practise riding the whole test too many times as your horse may anticipate movements and get ahead, rather than listening to you.

However, for the reluctant or nervous competitor, aim to ride it as many times as it takes for you to be confident enough to have a go. As you get happier entering, it may be that you don't need to over-practise the test and have enough confidence that you can ride all the elements required and put them together on the day. This is one for you to decide so do what works for you and change your plan as necessary as you progress. Even if you have a commander on the day, learn the test beforehand, practise riding individual parts of it and ride the whole test. On a windy day and/or with a lot of background noise you don't want to be left wondering where to go if you can't hear. Try to think of the commander as a back-up but not to be totally reliant on them.

Looking ahead gives you time to prepare for transitions and turns as well as allowing you to clearly see the markers. Looking ahead also helps with your posture and position. Do not tip forward locking your reins near your knees, it is not correct riding and the forced outline will not fool the judge. Notify your horse of an upcoming transition or turn by using the half-halt. This should also help to keep him balanced through the transition. Look where you are going, it will help the horse get there.

On a straight line you must make sure your horse is going actively forward in an even contact and good rhythm (don't allow him to rush). On the straights or up the centre line a horse that is not fully engaged and lacking impulsion will wobble and be more difficult to keep straight. Also, for the halt, ride in to the stop, don't just 'drop' the horse and amble to a finish looking relieved to have made it. Ride purposefully and as if you want to be there.

Use the time and distance between markers to your advantage. For example, use your space wisely, ask for the transition two or three strides after your horse has passed the first marker in the sequence so the judge can see that you are clearly past it but still have enough time to do what you need to do before the next one. If you ask for the transition half way between the markers or very late on as you approach the second you are doing yourself out of valuable time and may over-shoot the marker. This will lose you marks and may make you grab or rush slightly which will spoil the rhythm and make you look unprepared.

Ride a circle and not an egg by imagining it as a diamond shape where you join the four points together with a curve. Don't get lured onto the track for more than a stride or two if you are doing a circle. There needs to be a clear definition between a rider on the track and a rider doing a circle (particularly a 20-m circle where drifting on to the track forms a big temptation). Another way is to visualise the circle on the floor and ride it as if someone has sprayed it in coloured paint on to the floor. However you ride it ensure the horse is bent correctly around it with your legs guiding him.

The walk usually carries double marks so cash in on it. A judge wants to see a good stretch and a relaxed frame with a slightly longer stride. Don't just let go and allow the horse's head to drop abruptly down. Encourage him to take the contact down gently and stretch towards the ground. Encourage a forward, loose, swinging walk with your legs and pick up the contact gradually before you get to the next marker ready for the transition to the next movement.

The dressage arena has corners, so use them. Marks can be gained in a test where the corners are used rather than cutting them. Practise your corners so you know how deep in to them you can get before the horse loses his rhythm and balance and work on improving this element over time. All too often a horse has either no bend or is not bent correctly. Always make sure that your horse is bent slightly to the inside on circles, corners and turns. The saying 'inside leg to outside hand' should be in your mind. Don't be tempted to cross your hand over his neck or pull with the outside rein as you will get the wrong bend and he will lose balance.

Flexibility and self-carriage are what it is all about so a forced 'fake' outline is not the aim of the game here. Whatever your equestrian sport, this is a good rule to live by. When I ride a horse, I feel his way of going, I work to improve him, to flex him, moving and shaping him around my leg. It doesn't matter whether hacking or formal schooling, consistent training develops and strengthens the horse, gives him the physicality to perform and manoeuvre with lightness, suppleness and grace. Varying his work and training him sympathetically and consistently means he is not only fit physically but also fit mentally and eager to please. If you can do these things, no matter what discipline you are riding, you will have more chance of success in competition and every chance of enjoying your riding.

LETTER TO YOURSELF

This is a great way of looking at the reality of a situation, try doing one for yourself. This is my example letter.

Dear 'me',

Hey, not a great day, it's raining? Ok, so you know the rain will pass and after the rain, before you realise it the sun will shine again. Riding is like the weather, one day grey and drizzle, the next warm and sunny. Like all things that grow, you need both to flourish and become your best.

Remember that right now you are struggling to find the courage to compete, but sure as day turns to night, you will find the right way to go forward. All that seems scary now, will be the norm if you just pluck up the courage to enter one class. One class can become many classes and with this done, in the future, people will look to you for guidance and ask you how you do so well.

Keep the faith. The double oxer, the rein-back, the barrels, the trotting pole, the flying change or the correct canter lead may daunt you today, but in time, with perseverance and practise, you will crack it. Lateral movements or jumping the wings may seem a distant dream but by this time next year, or five years or ten years, you will no doubt be able to do the things you dream of so well that others will ask you for help in schooling. There's no rush and no time limit.

Remember the journey is varied but rich, so enjoy it. Yes, you can focus on the end result but make time each day to accept where you're at, take every day as it comes and remember to enjoy the progress you are making. However small it is, progress is still progress and of that you should always be proud.

Take time out for you, to love yourself and appreciate your life. Take time to love your horse and appreciate him for all he gives you. If he is a hairy pony or a gleaming thoroughbred, his heart is the same and his eagerness to please you a divine gift. Don't overlook his qualities in your hurry to perfect the exercises with which he struggles.

Don't lose your temper, it will only show you up and highlight your weaknesses. Be kind to your horse. If he isn't doing something correctly, teach him better. If you did or didn't go great at the show, keep your manners and be sportsman-like. If you don't over-react you will be welcomed back to try another day.

The wisdom you will give to others will read like this so live every word, do some things that scare you and for the sake of sanity, more things that don't. Bravery is not how high the fence is but what it means to you to jump it. Taking the stride is still taking the stride.

Show jumping is still show jumping whether its 30cm or 1m 30cm. Dressage is still dressage once you are on the centre line. Hacking is still hacking whether half a mile or 100 miles. Eventing is eventing once you compete all three phases. Showing is still showing once you are dressed up and in the ring. Never belittle your achievements, you are never 'only' or 'just'.

A horse cannot lie, try to be more like him. Don't let the pressure heaped upon you by others get too much. Apply yourself to all things you do but know when to draw the line and say enough is enough. You can try again tomorrow. Don't give up easily but don't be afraid to stop if you want to. Remember your trials, once you have achieved your goals, don't be mean about others who are still struggling. That was you once.

Have compassion and empathy in everything you do. Be positive and kind and it will always see you through. Never play down your achievements and never brag or boast either. Live life for you. We are only here once, this is not a dress rehearsal. Give it all you've got and in your older years, look back on all you achieved with affection and pride. The  rosettes and ribbons will fade, the memories will not. Cherish every moment with your horse and never stop trying or smiling.

Be proud of yourself, do your best and love your horse – always.

Lots of love,

Me x

DISPLAYING YOUR ROSETTES

This is just a bit of fun. A chance to focus on some lovely ways of displaying those hard-won rosettes as and when you get them and whether they read 1st or 'special'. Treasure them because they are the memories you have made. One day, if that horse isn't around anymore, or you are unable to ride, they may be the only physical thing you have to look back on, which I am sure you will do with great affection.

The box frame

A brilliant way of displaying rosettes, whether it is one big special championship beauty the size of a dinner plate on its own, or lots together in a bigger frame (if you can't buy a big enough one, get a local picture framer to do a bespoke one for you). Simply glue or use strong double sided tape on the back of the rosette to stick them to the coloured back board in the frame.  You will need to remove the metal hook or pin from the back but these usually pull out quite easily without damaging the rosette itself. The box frame will keep the rosettes dust and debris free for many years and if you hang it away from direct sunlight will stop them fading and protect them.

Perforated chipboard, thin metal sheets, acrylic etc

You can buy perforated light-weight materials from most DIY shops and simply thread some sturdy string or pretty ribbon through the top holes to hang it up or screw it to the wall using some of the pre-cut holes. It is then a case of simply using the rosette bridle hooks through the holes to display the rosettes in a way where they will not fall off but can be removed/re-arranged easily.

Perforated fabric

A great way of making a cheap, stylish, easy-to-arrange display is to use perforated fabric. Simply stitch or glue a bamboo cane, old curtain pole, dowel or similar rod across the top by folding the material over and attach some ribbon or string so you can hang it up. Push the rosettes into place by poking the bridle clip through the material.

Sashes

Sashes can be made into cushions or even wall hangings by stitching them together. These look fantastic and it is a great way of showing off those hard-earned championship moments.

I am sure there are hundreds of different ways from the basic hanging rosettes in a line on string to the most costly and elaborate methods. I am sure you will find the one that suits you and your budget. Be creative and whatever you come up with, I am sure it will bring you joy every time you look at your display.

If you come up with your own wonderful ideas for rosette displays, do share them with us on our Facebook group, we would love to see what you have come up with (type this in exactly)

Horse riders: nervous/anxious/lost confidence or use the link
https://m.facebook.com/groups/581906019359938/

CONCLUSION

Given that each person is different, there will always be systems which work for one person and not another. However, I have used the techniques in this book myself and with a number of nervous riders over the years. In addition, hundreds of people have benefited from my first book, *I Hope It Rains – the Confidence Manual for the nervous rider*. I feel passionately that this can help many others which is my one and only aim. There is a sea of confusion out there in the horse world when it comes to correct training and I hope that I have shed some light on what to look for in terms of gimmick-free, correct progressive approaches to competing and the journey as a whole. This in turn will help make you a more confident rider under pressure as well as having a well-schooled horse who is happy in his work.

There are elements of course which you have to understand and come to terms with as well as work hard at in order for these techniques to work effectively but you will conquer your anxieties in the end if you apply yourself properly. If you choose to ignore the full facts, approach the tasks half-heartedly or not give them your full attention, determination and commitment, you will get watered-down results. The ideas and techniques here can help you over the little stumbling blocks that are holding you back and stopping you doing things you want to do or being the best you can be.

So, however you choose to proceed, keep on track, keep in mind the competence/confidence equation and always try to keep your competition dreams in perspective. Seek the right help and learn to face your fears in a positive and constructive way. There is no shame in going back to basics and working through your issues slowly and surely. You need to be wise beyond your ego, pride or emotions. It is not always easy but success can only come from repetition and hard work and with some mental gymnastics you can achieve anything you put your mind to.

There will be good days and bad days along this journey but it is these ups and downs that make you a stronger person, more able to understand your horse, a better rider in the long term and hopefully, very importantly, a lot happier in general and in competition. Anyone who mucks out in extremely cold or blisteringly hot weather, spends every last penny they have on their horse and gives their love and time to these incredible animals deserves to ride and compete their horse without excessive anxiety.

Through my own journey I have tried to make that a reality and through this book point you in the right direction to help you achieve your dreams too. There is an element of 'face your fears and do it anyway', but with this system, I have found that it has worked time and time again, not just for major issues but for ironing out little creases in our riding as and when they appear. Practise, determination and honesty were key to unlocking my potential and I hope it helps you unlock yours.

Good luck x

DEDICATION

For my dear Nan. 1920 – 2020

To Andy Butcher (AB Equitation in Suffolk), for being a great horseman, fantastic trainer and one of the few who can make a horse truly dance. An inspirational, tough, no-nonsense instructor and I appreciate your support from backing to passage!

To Hannah for just being Hannah.

To Shaky, Prince, Sunny, Dublin, Polly, Hazel, Charlie, Tenko, Vienna, Tubby (aka Dubya G), Darling Flurry (Fluffy), Squirt, Rusty, Cohetta, Kalashnikov, Billy, Vaquera, Divatido and my beautiful, talented Helicon (aka King Zippy) for everything you taught me and continue to give me.

And to Patch, my amazing little cob who gave me thousands of miles of hacking until I found the courage to compete.

ABOUT THE AUTHOR

Born in 1973 I grew up in a small town called Oulton Broad in Suffolk. As a young girl, I was desperate to ride horses but not allowed. In hindsight, it just was never going to happen but at the time I had no clue and continued to pester my very non-horsey parents, oblivious to the fact that I wouldn't actually learn to ride until I was in my early twenties.

Those of you who have read my first book *I Hope It Rains, the Confidence Manual for the nervous rider,* will already know the story, but for those who don't, I was a relative late-comer to riding, taking it up in my early 20s. I went from a very keen, brave novice to being crippled with fear. Thankfully, due to the system I put together, I returned to being super-happy sitting on a horse and completely fear-free. I have shared the system for others in my books as I hope that my experiences can help many others suffering from nerves and anxiety to overcome them  and enjoy riding once again. Although I believe learning to ride later does set you up differently for your riding 'career', missing out on the 'Pony Club years' doesn't mean you can't be extremely proficient on a horse and learn to ride to a very high standard. I suppose anything we do as children may have advantages in terms of cementing it in our minds, but also has disadvantages as lessons taught may not have been correct and have remained unchallenged. An adult would question the rationale behind the instruction and seek the most knowledgeable person they could.

However, swings and roundabouts as it were, I think on the whole, you are aware as an adult of all the negatives that a child seems largely not to understand or, perhaps more accurately, not care about. I can assure you it wasn't all plain sailing, but without the ups and downs this book would not exist. For a number of years I worked as a professional rider with AB Film Horses in Suffolk but in terms of showing, dressage, *doma vaquera*, working equitation and distance riding I ride and compete for fun as an amateur. Through years of hard work and sometimes hard knocks, I am able to feel confident and competent with horses both mounted and on the ground. This is due to good tuition from my former employer, who is still my trainer and mentor with all things horsey and, on my part, due to hours spent in the saddle, persistence and hard work.

I quickly learned there is no quick fix or magic (unfortunately) when it comes to correct horse training. I have completed over 1500 recorded distance riding miles so far, schooled, drag-hunted and jumped my way through my horsey life and hopefully will continue to do so for many, many years yet. I have been incredibly lucky to have ridden very highly trained stunt, trick and film horses as well as magnificent Haute École and Grand Prix dressage and jumping horses. These have given me the tools I needed to introduce and successfully compete my young horse (my little 'Ferrari'), as well as continuing to enjoy hacking and distance riding on my mare who, despite her tricky, grumpy demeanour, crosses country like a steam train and is one of my best and most loyal friends.

I have been very fortunate to ride under instruction from former World and European Champions as well as being taught in the main by Horse Master Andy Butcher. He not only trains horses to the highest level for Hollywood films, but is an incredible trainer in the more usual disciplines of dressage and working equitation. One thing these individuals have in common, despite being riding masters, is that they are still willing to help the amateur rider and unreservedly give their knowledge and tuition to anyone willing to listen, learn and grow.

I live for my three beautiful horses and each day remain thankful for the lessons they teach me and the joy that just seeing them over the stable door brings to my head, my heart and my soul.

CREDITS, THANKS AND RESOURCES

AB Equitation – horse breaking and training from backing to Grand Prix.
www.abequitation.co.uk

Sarah Cameron – for your much appreciated expert eye and editing.

Ronnie Hall Sports Hypnotherapy, Suffolk. For helping me fine tune my mind allowing me to enjoy competing.

Kinesiology: to find a registered practitioner, go to
www.kinesiologyfederation.co.uk

Images:
Editing: Vincipie (Fiverr.com)
Cover Stars – Hannah, Sarah, Liz and Lily.
Photo Credits: H Ellis, E Moore, S Harding, L Golding-Smith, Picklejar pictures, Equimages, A Butcher, F Smither (cover).
Hands courtesty of Free Images online.

*Amazon best seller - July 2020 in Equine & Sport.

Please visit my friendly Facebook group for kind, non-judgemental chat and advice (type this exactly)

Horse riders: nervous/anxious/lost confidence
https://m.facebook.com/groups/581906019359938/

Or my page: **https://m.facebook.com/confidentriderhuo/**

**Or my website:
www.confident-rider.co.uk**

Books in the series by the same author:

I HOPE IT RAINS – The Confidence Manual for the nervous rider
Available on Amazon. ISBN: 9798631689312

The complete confidence manual for the nervous rider. Practical, realistic advice and workable plans to overcome your fear and deal effectively with your anxiety whilst taking small, positive steps to achieve your goals and enjoy riding your horse. Whatever your chosen discipline, from hacking to jumping, this book can help you realise your full potential. Never again will you 'hope it rains' so you don't have to ride your horse! Boost your confidence and enjoy riding, whatever the situation, whatever the weather.

A note from me to you: I have had a lifelong passion for horses with immense enjoyment and success but have also experienced a time when my nerves almost got the better of me. I wrote this book to help others overcome their fear whilst controlling negative, self-limiting beliefs. It makes me so very sad to see people not enjoying their equine friends and I hope to help you overcome your problems and let you re-discover your love of riding. Today is a great day to start living your dreams...

Readers' comments:

Mrs A S Simpson: "Buy this book... borrow this book... definitely READ this book... it could change your life, your understanding of fear, change your everything!"

Mrs J Wickett: "Best book I have ever read, it has helped me so much. Thank you, Thank you, Thank you".

Miss S A Earle: "Brilliant, practical tools to help everyone achieve".

Amazon Customer (verified purchase): "Cannot recommend this book enough. Has allowed me to chase the demons which were holding me back… Simple, easy to understand and follow. Thank you".

Shelly (Amazon Verified Purchase): "Brilliant, so easy to follow and understand".

Jay (via personal message):- "This book saved me from myself, I beat my demons and now can enjoy my riding again, with no fears or nerves at all. I can't thank you enough."

Printed in Great Britain
by Amazon